D0853331

2004
for the love of books & the hope to inspire
this book is donated by
Dr. Charles L. Foster
Brandon, VT 05733

ACHIEVING
PERSONAL
GREATNESS

ACHIEVING

PERSONAL

GREATNESS

DISCOVER THE 10 POWERFUL KEYS TO UNLOCKING YOUR POTENTIAL

TIM LAVENDER

THOMAS NELSON PUBLISHERS®
Nashville

A Division of Thomas Nelson, Inc.
www.ThomasNelson.com

Copyright © 2002 by Tim Lavender

All rights reserved. No portion of this book may be reproduced, stored in a retrieval system, or transmitted in any form or by any means—electronic, mechanical, photocopy, recording, or other—except for brief quotations in printed reviews, without the prior permission of the publisher.

Published in Nashville, Tennessee, by Thomas Nelson, Inc.

All Scripture quotations are taken from the NEW KING JAMES VERSION®. Copyright © 1979, 1980, 1982 by Thomas Nelson, Inc. Used by permission. All rights reserved.

Library of Congress Cataloging-in-Publication Data

Lavender, Tim.
    Achieving personal greatness : discover the 10 powerful keys to unlocking your potential / Tim Lavender.
      p. cm.
    ISBN 0-7852-6556-2
    1. Self-actualization (Psychology) I. Title.
BF637.S4 L395 2002
158.1—dc21   2002006423

Printed in the United States of America

1 2 3 4 5 6 BVG 06 05 04 03 02

DEDICATION

To the three great mentors who have shaped my life—Donny, Larry, and Michael. Thank you for using your positive influence to unlock my potential.

To my best friend and wife, Joy. Thank you for believing in me when I was all alone. Your unconditional love has energized my life like nothing else ever could.

To my dear children, Jacob and Rachel. You are my greatest gifts from the hand of God.

CONTENTS

Unlock the Greatness Inside You

One Saturday when I was thirteen years old, my best friend invited me to play golf with him. At that time, I was an avid and successful baseball player and, generally speaking, an excellent athlete, but I had never picked up a golf club. My friend, on the other hand, had played golf with his dad every weekend for a couple of years.

I picked up the clubs with the same ten-finger grip I used in baseball and slugged away . . . and after eighteen holes, I had a better score than my friend. I had also fallen in love with the game.

I played golf as often as I was able and slowly but steadily lowered my score. Then I hit a plateau. I was determined to continue to improve, but nothing I tried seemed to help. I sought out a pro at a local club and signed up for a lesson.

The pro took one look at my swing and promptly advised me that the ten-finger grip I had used to hold a baseball bat didn't work in golf, and that I would need to change my grip if I wanted to play better golf. He showed me the proper grip, and I swung away. Nothing about that grip felt comfortable. The ball didn't go nearly as far or in the direction I desired. After half a bucket of balls with the new swing, I informed the pro that I couldn't make the change.

I expected him to offer a Plan B approach to improving my game, but to my surprise, he said, "OK, That's all for today."

I was stunned. "All for today? You mean the lesson is over?" I asked.

"Yes," he said.

"But why? That's all you're going to teach me in one lesson?"

The pro responded, "If you don't change your grip, you're as good as you'll ever be. Nothing else I tell you will matter if you don't change your grip."

I wanted to improve in golf more than I wanted to cling to my old habits, so I made the change. As awkward as it was at first, as unsuccessful as I was at first, as clumsy as the new grip felt at first, I made the change. I practiced and practiced until I could hit the ball with the new grip as well as I had with my old baseball-style grip. And then I began to hit the ball even *better*.

Years later, I'm still hitting the ball with the proper grip, and I'm still in love with the game. I've won fifteen amateur tournaments, and I hope to win more.

If you truly want to unlock the potential for greatness that lies within you, you are going to have to make some changes in the way you think. Perhaps the first change needs to be in the way you think about personal greatness.

EMBRACE YOUR OWN GREATNESS

A friend of mine said to me, "You know, I'm not sure about your idea of personal greatness. It sort of makes me feel uncomfortable to tell someone that I think I can be great."

"Really?" I said. "You know, I knew your father, and in some ways, he was the father I never really had. How do you evaluate your dad? How do you rate him when it comes to being great?"

"Oh, Dad was a great man. No doubt about it! I learned so many things from him," he replied.

"What about our mutual friend John? You and I have enjoyed his friendship for many years. What about him?" I asked.

"Oh, he has been a great friend to me," he said. "I think he's a great guy."

"Well, if these people are great in your eyes, don't you believe you can be great in the eyes of others?"

I watched his face closely as I asked this question. It was as if a light went on.

Personal greatness is not about your believing that you can achieve superiority over others. It's not about developing a proud attitude. It's not about being better than other people.

Personal greatness is about your becoming foundation-ally great and great in the eyes of others so that one thing might happen—they might be influenced to be more than they would be without you in their lives.

We seem to use the term *great* all the time. We talk about great friends and the great times we share with them. We talk about the great teachers we have had over the years and how they influenced our lives. We talk about great pastors we have had, great courses we have taken, great books we have read, great movies we have seen, great songs we have heard, great things we have experienced, and great lessons we have learned.

The idea of greatness is common to us, and we use it to describe people and things that have had a positive influence on our lives. However, most of us don't use the term *great* to describe ourselves.

In my nearly three decades of being in business and working with all types of people, I have learned that many, if not most, people believe deep down inside that they can be great. There is a still, small voice telling them that they can be someone special. It's the inner greatness—the inner desire to be one's very best—that is at the heart of personal greatness.

Personal greatness has nothing to do with being exceptionally intelligent, rich, famous, or politically successful. It's about being a person who exerts *positive influence* on others. Personal greatness is a matter of unlocking your potential and using your potential in such a way that it overflows into other people's lives to generate a positive result.

This book presents three basic laws of personal greatness, seven guiding principles that are absolutely necessary for you to embrace if you are to unlock your potential, and ten powerful keys that can help you release your potential and turn it into positive influence. Together, these laws, principles, and keys present the way to achieve your very own expression of personal greatness.

I invite you to the adventure.

I invite you to take a step toward the day when other people will call you great because of the wonderful things you have helped unlock in their lives.

THE 3 BASIC LAWS
OF PERSONAL GREATNESS

POTENTIAL PLUS POSITIVE INFLUENCE PRODUCES PERSONAL GREATNESS

WHEN I WAS WORKING ON MY MASTER'S DEGREE IN business administration at Southern Methodist University, I had a leadership professor who made this claim in a lecture: "Hitler was a great leader." Most of us in the class grimaced. He went on, however, to ask us to argue in *favor* of that statement. Some of the arguments that emerged were these:

- Great leaders have lots of followers. Hitler certainly had lots of followers.

- Great leaders rise to positions of great power. Hitler certainly did.

- Great leaders control the lives of many people. Hitler certainly controlled the lives of many people—those loyal to him as well as his archenemies.

- Great leaders fill a void in history. They are born into leadership or made leaders by historical circumstances.

An argument could be made that Hitler came to leadership in a narrow window of Germany's history that "allowed" him to be a leader.

Hitler fills traditional claims about leadership on all accounts. But was he truly a *great* leader? Nobody in the class was willing to give him that acclaim.

Such arguments tend to emerge and support a theory that leadership is *positional*. Positional leadership theories are always related to issues of power and control, and they are always related to an organization of some type—whether the organization is an entire nation, culture, religion, or corporation.

I don't believe that leadership is merely positional, but even more so, I don't believe that personal greatness is at all positional. In other words, a person is not great because he is in a position of having the most, doing the most, being the top in his field, or head of the company. The foremost reason my fellow students did not want to describe Hitler as a great leader was rooted in their belief that Hitler was not a great *person*. And the reasons he was not considered a great person had nothing to do with position, power, number of followers, or place in history.

Is there another aspect to greatness?

I strongly believe there is.

CONFRONTING THE FOUR GREAT MYTHS OF PERSONAL GREATNESS

Through the years, I have routinely encountered four claims—which I call myths—about personal greatness:

1. Great people are born, not made.

2. Great people are made by circumstances.

3. Great people have magnetic personalities.

4. Great leaders exert power and control.

At the very outset of this book, let me give you my response to these myths.

Myth #1: *Great People Are Born, Not Made*

Becoming a great person is a learning and growing process, not a one-time event and not an achievable status. Some people begin to exercise their potential and manifest influence early on. We tend to think of these people as being born leaders or born with greatness. In truth, they were not born into greatness. Rather, they were taught or influenced early in life as to *how* a person should lead a successful life, and they began early their journey toward personal greatness. The good news, however, is that those who do not begin this process early in life can and often do begin this process later in life.

I strongly believe personal greatness is forged. Greatness is learned, developed, and practiced. Achieving personal greatness is a process available to every person.

Those who believe great people are born also tend to believe that only a select few are designated by fate to become leaders; the rest of us are followers. Leadership is often presented as a model in which one person is out front or on top of the organizational pyramid; all others are on the lower levels of the pyramid as followers. This view of leadership is *positional*. It is exclusive to a few. It is a matter of power, position, and control.

In contrast, I contend that every person is born with both the capacity and the challenge to lead. Every person is born with talents, an ability to learn, a personality, and an opportunity to grow. If leaders are born, then the logical conclusion must be that those born to lead will eventually rise to leadership. Not everybody, however, turns innate talents, capacities, abilities, and opportunities into strong character. And not everybody applies skills and abilities into useful and positive service to others.

All *can* achieve personal greatness. Not all *choose* to become personally great.

All *can* become leaders. Not all *choose* to become leaders.

Myth #2: Great People Are Made by Circumstances

I do not believe great people or great leaders are made by the times in which they live or the circumstances in which they find themselves. Rather, they are made to the extent that they choose to make the most of what they have been given, choose to bless others to the greatest ability they have to give, and choose to respond to circumstances with the most energetic exercise of their potential and the most compassionate and positive influence they can exert.

There are those who contend that only certain types of people can rise to genuine leadership. For them, leaders are made by the circumstances of their abilities. In other words, people with great ability become leaders. One prominent leadership expert once said, "You can take a leader and train him to manage, but you can never take a manager and train him to lead." Again, I strongly disagree. That may be a man's theory, but it isn't the truth. Every person can learn how to lead.

I visualize the process of achieving personal greatness in this way. It starts with opening a large and powerful door, beyond which lies a marvelous pathway. The journey along this pathway lasts a lifetime. There are steps and stages to negotiate along the way, there are decisions to make at various forks in the road, and there is the effort of walking and the perseverance to continue walking when obstacles appear in the path. But the journey is there for all who will open the door and walk the path.

Myth #3: Great People Have Magnetic Personalities

People with great personalities are fun to be around. They can be energizing and motivating. It's a good thing to have a great personality! The danger, however, for those with magnetic personalities is that they tend to rely on feedback from those around them, and they tend to play to the audience that gives them the most enthusiastic applause. The end result is that they are led by the very masses they are attempting to lead.

A person may be born with a magnetic personality and many gifts. Yet there is no automatic guarantee that such a person will be a great person or a leader. Conversely a person may have a fairly dull personality and only a single gift, but such a person can still achieve personal greatness—and such a person can still become a leader.

Myth #4: Great Leaders Exert Power and Control

The amazing thing about this myth is that it is usually voiced by those who admit—albeit under pressure sometimes—that they are victims of those who exert or are attempting to exert power and control over their lives. People who do not feel themselves bound or limited by a powerful, controlling authority figure rarely hold to this myth.

Personal greatness is not about the number of people who follow you or who are beneath you on an organizational chart. Personal greatness is about knowing who you are, living out your key purpose in life, and influencing as many people as you can for good through willing service and generous giving of yourself.

A New Approach to Personal Greatness

Personal greatness is about potential and influence. It is not about how powerful a position you may achieve or about how many people you may supervise or have in your "camp." Real greatness is about how much of your personal potential you actually achieve and how positive an influence you have upon people in your life.

I advocate this model:

Potential + Positive Influence = Personal Greatness

Most people will never be the leader of a large company or fill a state or national political office. Most people will never play on a world championship team or gain worldwide recognition. Most people will not play on the world stage in a leadership capacity.

The average person is not going to exert great power or control over a large group of people. Every person, however,

can be a great leader of himself and those within his immediate circle of family, friends, and colleagues.

Every person has personal potential and the privilege of
influencing others. *Every* person will encounter literally
thousands of people over a lifetime and will have the opportunity to impact their lives in some way. *Every* person will
have the opportunity to inspire or motivate others to pursue
their personal potential and passions.

POTENTIAL IS DYNAMIC AND EVER-GROWING

Potential is not a static concept. Potential is the composite
set of talents and skills that a person has at any given time.
Each person is born with a measure of potential (some small,
some great)—it is his or her starting point. Very often, that
potential is first recognized by objective observers, such as
parents, grandparents, teachers, pastors, and others in the
young child's life. To a certain extent, a child first learns of
his potential by hearing others tell him that he has, or does
not have, potential. The child also has an understanding that
he is capable of doing some things—in fact, from a child's
perspective, he usually believes he is capable of doing *all*
things, even flying like a bird and catching speeding bullets.

For many years, I held to the concept that potential was a
vast pool of some type—a little like a lake that had a bottom so
deep you couldn't see it from the surface. Potential was there to
be explored and pursued, but it was a fixed entity. Given enough
time and energy put to the task, a person could come close to
mapping out the full extent of his potential over the course of a

lifetime. This is why Tiger Woods, who has greatly released his potential, feels like he can become better and better.

In recent years, my concept of potential has shifted dramatically. I now contend that potential is an unfolding concept. The more we exercise and use the talents we were given at birth and the skills we have developed since birth, the greater the potential for further discovering and developing our talents and skills! There is no end or arrival point in the journey toward our potential.

An analogy might be drawn to a growing awareness and understanding of the concept of the horizon. If you are living in a forest, you have little concept of the horizon. You see only blotches of sky overhead. As you move into more expansive territory, perhaps higher up the mountain or into a large meadow or valley, you have a better concept of the horizon. You continue to move toward it. Even higher up the mountain, or farther out into the plains, you have a better concept of the horizon. It becomes even more vast, more compelling, and more exhilarating as it beckons to you.

Potential will result in these desires:

- The more you see, the more you want to see.

- The more you do, the more you want to do.

- The more you discover you are capable of accomplishing, the more you want to accomplish and the more you want to discover your hidden talents.

- The more you learn, the more you want to learn.

- The more you succeed in one area of your life, the more you want to succeed in all areas of your life.

- The deeper a loving relationship grows, the more you want to pursue that relationship and explore the full depths of it.

Potential drives us forward. It compels us to act and to grow and to explore. Potential *energizes* us.

A friend once said to me that in the course of pursuing his doctorate, he found himself coming to this conclusion: "The more I studied, the more I knew what I didn't know and the more enthusiastic and driven I felt to learn. In the end, I stood before my doctoral committee with a very humble declaration, 'I know nothing, but I have a library card and I know a little better where to look for what I still want to know.' In the end, that was probably the exact place in which my committee wanted me to be—humbly stupid but eager to do the research they had equipped me to do."

That's potential! The more we see ourselves objectively and yet optimistically, the more we see what we can be and the more eager we are to embark on a journey of self-discovery and self-actualization. Those who seek personal greatness—those who desire to achieve personal leadership of themselves—are energized by what they *are not, have not, and cannot do . . . yet.* Put a huge emphasis on that word *yet.*

Those who seek personal greatness are wildly optimistic and deeply challenged by their capacities and capabilities that remain to be realized, fulfilled, and exercised. They are not in the least discouraged by what they cannot do; rather, they are motivated to turn the things they cannot do into things they *can* do. They desire to be all they can be and all they believe it is wise and good to be.

As young children, how many of us said, "Look, Mom, look,

Dad, look at what I can be and do"? That's the lifelong attitude of those who seek personal greatness. They are not in the least bit daunted by the vastness of the challenge that lies in their immediate future. They are energized to take on the imminent challenge because beyond it they see the vastness of their potential.

CONSCIOUS REFLECTION AND EFFORT

We do not wander casually into our potential. The pursuit of potential takes effort. It takes conscious, active reflection and exploration of our talents. We need to discover the things at which we are innately good. We need to acknowledge what triggers our imaginations and excites us to the point of setting goals. We need to understand what motivates us. And once we discover our dreams and recognize our talents, we need to turn those dreams into plans and those talents into skills.

Most, if not all, of the principles and keys presented later in this book are aimed at helping you recognize and exercise your potential and then maximize it through a recognition of your dreams and talents, guiding principles, and the development of related skills.

POSITIVE INFLUENCE COMPELS CHANGE

We simply do not live or work in a vacuum. Even those who are unmarried, who have no children, and who work at home are not truly alone. John Donne said it as well as any person ever has: "No man is an island."

We live in relationship to other people, and we exert either a positive or a negative influence on every person we encounter—from stranger to intimate confidant, from casual acquaintance to spouse, from the person we met yesterday at a business conference to the friend we have known since childhood.

Our influence may be temporary or short lived, or it may be abiding and long term.

Our influence may be casual or minor, or it may be profoundly life altering.

Our influence may be immediately felt, or it may not be recognized until after our deaths.

Our influence may be in the physical and material realm, or it may be exerted in the emotional, intellectual, or spiritual realm.

Influence is the ability to prompt change in another person. It may be the ability to change circumstances around the person, motivate the person to change his circumstances, or encourage the person to change his way of thinking, believing, or responding.

In all cases, our influence prompts positive growth, development, and change in another person, or it prompts something negative, destructive, diminishing, or limiting.

You may ask, "What about the person who has no influence one way or another?"

I don't believe that's possible. You will help a person in some way, or you will hinder a person in some way.

I heard a bus driver say about one of his passengers, "I really like that guy."

"Do you know him?" I asked.

"Not really," he said. "But he's been riding my bus for about six months now."

"If you don't really know him, then how do you know you like him?"

"Well, he always has his money ready when he gets on board, and he always says 'good morning' to me with a smile on his face."

"So," I said, "he doesn't slow you down by slowing down other passengers, and he's a source of positive encouragement?"

"Yeah," the bus driver said with a laugh. "I guess you could put it that way. Are you a professor or something?"

"Sorta," I said. "I'm interested in whether people are a positive or a negative influence on others."

"Oh, he's a positive," the man said again with a chuckle. "I wish all my passengers were as positive. There's just something about that guy that makes me feel good. He brings a smile to my soul."

Great people do bring smiles to the souls of other people. They energize people with the energy they are putting into their pursuit of personal greatness. They encourage by word and by example. They compel positive change. They exert *influence*.

Being a positive influence on another person may not be something of which we are conscious. I suspect the passenger in question never had a clue about what that bus driver thought of him. Nevertheless, he qualified as a positive influence.

We all seem to be attracted to people who are in pursuit of their potential. I certainly am. Those who are pursuing their potential with energy and enthusiasm emit a strong drawing power. They are compelling, magnetic people you feel good being around. They are people you almost unwittingly follow, if for no reason other than to see what they will say next, do next, enjoy next, explore next, experience next. Those who are pursuing personal greatness inevitably exert leadership, even if they are not seeking to be a "leader." Leadership is a by-product of great personal influence.

THE CHALLENGE OF INFLUENCE

The challenge before us, then, is to seek to be a positive influence to all people we encounter—all the time.

We need to use our talents and skills to help others in some way; we can encourage, assist, bless, inform, build up, and promote others. We can help other people feel more positive about themselves by expressing words of genuine compliment, appreciation, and thankfulness.

We also need to understand that we owe it to ourselves to be a positive influence on ourselves. We can influence ourselves by thinking and speaking positively about our accomplishments, talents, skills, and character qualities. There's nothing to be gained by calling ourselves—or thinking of ourselves—as stupid, lazy, inept, failures, or limited in any way. Conversely, there's a great deal to be gained by thinking and speaking of ourselves as trained, ready, willing, capable, eager, enthusiastic, and actively pursuing a limitless life. Certainly I am not advocating prideful boasting or public pronouncement of one's greatness or ability. Rather, I am advocating a positive self-acknowledgment of our current levels of potential.

How do you see yourself today?

What words would you use to define or describe yourself?

How do you think about yourself?

I like to read my Bible every day as a source of energy and wisdom. The Bible teaches about mankind: "A good man out of the good treasure of his heart brings forth good; and an evil man out of the evil treasure of his heart brings forth evil. For out of the abundance of the heart his mouth speaks" (Luke 6:45).

If you don't particularly like how you see yourself today—how you define or describe yourself or how you envision yourself in your heart—change what you see, think, or envision. Change the definition of your inner life! The change begins on the inside, not by overt actions.

Begin to see yourself as the self you desire to be.

Begin to envision yourself displaying the character you would like to manifest.

Begin to think of yourself in the terms by which you would like for others to describe you.

One of the best-known motivational teachers of the past century suggested that every person make an appointment with "self" at least once a week—a set time for sitting and reflecting for at least fifteen minutes on "the me I want to be." This time for reflection is to be done in quiet solitude.

I chose to do this for several months, and I found it an amazing technique. To reconnect every week with the person I wanted to be—to reflect upon the character I wanted to develop in my life, the traits I wanted to manifest, the abilities and skills I wanted to pursue, the dreams I wanted to realize—caused me to focus my efforts and direct my energy toward the things that truly mattered most to me. I highly recommend this practice to you.

FIND A SOURCE OF AFFIRMATION AND ENCOURAGEMENT

A positive influence flows directly from receiving positive influence from others. You can generate some positive influence in your strength and confidence. Most of your ability to exercise positive influence, however, comes from your receiving the positive influence from an outside source of inspiration. When a parent affirms you as a worthy, talented, beloved child, you regard other people as being worthy, talented, and beloved. When a teacher tells you that you are having a good impact on others, you seek new ways to be a person who influences others for good. When a coach says that you are a key player and "a team member important for morale," you play harder and seek to display more team spirit. When you know deep within your heart that you are loved by God, you are more willing to love the unlovable people you encounter. When you know deep within your heart that you are forgiven by God, you find that you are more willing to forgive others.

What if you don't have someone exerting positive influence on your life? Find a source of positive influence!

Build new, positive friendships or mentoring relationships. Find someone who can coach you, train you, teach you, motivate you, or build you up. Choose to associate with people who energize you. Personal greatness can be "caught" as well as "taught." Listen to people who speak words that you find inspiring, encouraging, and growth producing. Read books, listen to tapes, attend seminars, take courses, or engage in volunteer opportunities so you may grow as a person. Seek out the best influences on your life. What you take in will directly affect what you dish out.

You can never make a good product using inferior parts or ingredients.

You can never teach a person what you don't know.

You can never model behavior for a person unless you have seen it modeled for you.

You can never have a winning team with players who see themselves as losers.

Choose to be around winners and producers and successful people. Choose to be around givers and encouragers. Choose to be around those who have faith, hope, and a charitable spirit. Choose to open yourself up to receiving what others desire to give freely. Choose to associate with those who manifest the virtue and character that you admire and that you desire to develop in your life. And choose to give back from the treasury of all that has been poured into you.

Just as potential is not static, neither is positive influence. Your positive influence grows as you avail yourself of the opportunity to be *influenced*. (Many of the keys presented later in this book elaborate on this theme of influence.)

A Leader Versus a Follower

Achieving personal greatness ultimately requires combining the "being" side of your life—your potential and the actualization and development of your values, talents, and skills—with the "doing" side of your life—the activities and behaviors that exert influence.

The pursuit of personal greatness begins with self, but it never ends with self. If you are actively pursuing your talents and are turning them into skills, if you are seeking to have a positive influence on others, then you are going to be a leader in somebody's eyes.

First, you are going to see yourself as leading yourself. You are going somewhere. You are becoming today more than you were yesterday—by intention, by effort, by learning, by practice. You are going somewhere—you are headed toward your future with a goal, a plan, and a purpose. You are exerting active influence on what you think, on how you respond to life's challenges, on what you choose to take into your life, and on the relationships you choose to develop in your life.

You are not simply going with the flow, ending up wherever the slow-moving river of life takes you. Instead, you are mapping out a course that will take you down the river efficiently, effectively, and safely. You are not simply taking life as it comes; rather, you are embracing all life holds out to you, and you are pursuing the fullness of life with energy, vision, and purpose.

Perhaps one of the best ways to understand what it means to be a leader is to take a brief look at what it means to be a follower. A follower

- follows the crowd. He does what others are doing or what others tell him to do.

- follows his nose. He does what is immediately in front of him with no forethought of the future.

- follows his emotions. He does what feels good at any particular moment, with little concern for consequences, personal growth, or the development of his potential.

- follows the lead of others. He takes a job because it is

offered rather than looking at the way that job both fits and challenges his innate talents; he joins a club because he is asked to join instead of considering how that club's purposes reflect his purpose in living.

- follows the path of least resistance. He does not actively seek out the things that demand intellectual, emotional, or spiritual growth.

A follower generally pays little attention to those who may be looking to him for direction. He openly declares, "I'm not a role model, I don't want to be a role model, so don't expect me to be a role model." In truth, everybody is a role model to somebody—there's no escaping that fact. Everybody is a role model of what to do or what not to do.

A follower intuitively knows that his children are likely to follow in his footsteps, but he gives little thought to what that may mean. He takes the attitude of "live and let live," yet he does very little to better his life or to further the ability of others to live a quality life. A follower does not see himself as a leader—a leader of himself or a leader of anybody else.

The exact opposite is true of a genuine leader. A leader who manifests personal greatness

- determines the right path to follow personally, and then walks out that path.

- thinks about tomorrow. He sets goals and makes plans to get to the place he wants to be.

- recognizes that he has the potential always for influencing others, and he seeks to influence others for good.

- weighs affiliations, memberships, and opportunities in the light of their ability to help him become the person he wants to be. He intentionally pursues opportunities and relationships that he believes will be mutually beneficial for the accomplishment of worthy goals.

A leader actively leads his own life. And in so doing, he provides leadership by example to others.

INFLUENTIAL EXAMPLE OFTEN RESULTS IN POSITIONAL LEADERSHIP

What is the relationship between influential leadership and positional leadership? Well, the truth is this: those who provide leadership by example tend to be those who are promoted or pushed into positional leadership by those they influence.

I have seen people put into positional leadership roles because they had familial or political connections—in other words, other people set them up to do a job to bring benefit to themselves—or because they had more skills than their peers. Such positional leaders may be able to do a job, but they are rarely followed willingly or eagerly by others, and they are never truly given accolades of "great," "worthy," "honored," "respected," "noble," or "admired."

On the other hand, I have never seen a person who was exerting great positive influence and was actively pursuing potential (turning talents into skills and dreams into plans) fail to be elevated to a greater position at some point. It may be the position of matriarch or patriarch in the family, a leadership role in a church or ministry, a greater rank in the organization, or a title such as team captain, group leader, or block chairman.

In other words, not all positional leaders are those we elevate in our hearts and minds as being our personal leaders and role models. But all genuinely influential leaders—all those who achieve personal greatness—become positional leaders. Perhaps not immediately, but eventually. Perhaps not with a dramatic rise on the corporate ladder, but certainly in the greater fabric of their social and cultural and spiritual milieu. Their personal energy, dreams, and pursuit of excellence act like a magnet that attracts others to follow their example, to emulate their character, to sign up for their causes, to align themselves with their parties, to associate with their concerns, and to seek to spend time in their presence. Those who follow such people may not fully understand or recognize that they are following—nonetheless, they are following, they are influenced, and they are being led.

One of the most remarkable examples of this model of leadership was Mother Teresa. She spent much of her life on the streets of Calcutta. She had been a teacher, and she knew that the best teachers teach by their example, so that's what she did. She taught people how to have compassion for the dying poor, and how to help them die with dignity.

She never strayed from this message, even when she traveled outside Calcutta. The purpose for her sharing her message elsewhere was to talk about the need to show compassion for disenfranchised, sick, lonely, dying, helpless people. She raised millions upon millions of dollars for that cause and energized a large group of full-time "sisters" as well as others who would do the work and raise the money necessary to fund the work long after her death.

Mother Teresa affected lives around the world with her simple message that was backed up by her personal example of effort and character. She had tremendous positive influence, she released her potential, and she changed her world. Was she a great leader? Did she achieve personal greatness? I don't know very many people who would say anything other than "Absolutely!"

THREE QUESTIONS WORTHY OF REFLECTION

If you are truly going to move toward personal greatness, you need to ask yourself today:

1. *Am I willing to recognize and embrace the fact that I have been created with great potential that is not yet activated or actualized? Am I willing to define and pursue my potential?*

2. *Am I willing to recognize and embrace the fact that I can and do exert influence on others? Am I willing to direct my energies toward manifesting a positive influence on others?*

3. *Am I willing to take full responsibility for who I am, and to allow what I do to flow from who I am? Am I willing to take charge of my life, choosing to lead my life rather than be led by others?*

I hope your answers are all a resounding "Yes!"

LAW #2

POTENTIAL IS GREATER
THAN POWER

A NUMBER OF YEARS AGO A MAN I'LL CALL JAMES AND I were working for the same organization in two separate divisions. James was the CEO of a start-up subsidiary company. Previously he had worked for a major distribution company in a related field, and prior to that, he had held a major marketing position for a Fortune 500 company. I say all that to indicate he was well qualified for his new CEO position. He is a very talented young man.

We had lunch together one day, sitting out on a park bench in a lovely town square. James said, "I just came out of a meeting where I was told, 'You aren't CEO material, and that is why this subsidiary company is not moving forward.'"

"What prompted that?" I asked.

He said, "I was unwilling to sign a larger line-of-credit loan at the bank. I've already signed a line-of-credit loan for $200,000. These loans have to be secured by my personal collateral. I sold my home and moved into a house half the size—which I'm renting, not purchasing—just so I would feel comfortable signing the first loan. I don't feel comfortable going beyond the credit line already in place."

He then went on to say, "What these executives of the parent company said to me really rocked me. What do you think I should do?"

I could certainly understand his reluctance to extend himself further and the blow that their criticism had leveled.

"What do you think you should do with your life?" I asked. "Not today or tomorrow, but ultimately."

We sat on that park bench talking at length, and he shared some of the personal dreams and goals he had for his life.

I responded, "On the basis of what you have told me, I think you should resign."

"When?" he said.

"Today."

"Are you serious?" he asked.

"Yes," I said. "Based upon what you have told me, and assuming you have been honest with yourself and with me, and you have an accurate perception of what happened to you this morning, I think you should resign."

James did resign—not that day, but within a week.

I knew at the time we talked that I was speaking not only to James but also to myself. I was not truly doing, at that point and in that position, what I ultimately wanted to do with my life. I resigned from my position a month later.

Shortly after I resigned, I had a call from James. He asked, "What are you doing?"

I said, "Sitting here trying to figure out the next step I want to take."

"I'm doing the same thing," he said. "Why don't we meet and figure this out together?"

We did meet. And that afternoon, James wrote out the vision he had for a company of his own, and I wrote out the vision for the company I established.

James and I had reached the point in our lives where we realized that we had been letting other people define us as individuals—and in the process, letting them define for us our careers and setting for us a ceiling on how high and how far we could go.

Are you in a similar situation today?

Are you defining your own life, or are you letting the opinions of others shape how you think about yourself? James had been told, "You aren't CEO material," and he almost internalized that by thinking, *Perhaps I'm not CEO material. Perhaps I'm not cut out for this.* When James began to define himself, and act on the basis of his personal definitions for himself, he was willing to take a risk, step out on his own, and start a company—as CEO, by the way!

A second key thing happened out of my meeting with James. As part of our discussion that afternoon, each of us noted the other's personal core talents and skills. James saw some talents in me that I hadn't fully seen in myself—but that I intuitively knew to be true the moment he named those talents. I also saw some talents in him that he hadn't fully seen in himself, but that he knew to be true.

In isolating and identifying our core talents, the next step for our lives seemed to flow almost automatically. We created pathways for our lives that were totally in keeping with our talents. James went down one path—and I, another. James turned out to be one of the finest CEOs I've ever encountered. I am doing what I know is totally in keeping with who I am.

What James and I did that day was, to a great extent, to activate areas of potential in our lives that had been dormant. We began to revisit our deepest dreams and focus on our highest purpose for being.

POTENTIAL IS FRAMED BY YOUR DREAMS

We dream about our lives, especially the future. We "live" in the future we hold in our minds. It is the very real place we hope to occupy someday in the not-too-distant future.

Dreams are a reflection of the hope that is built within every person, regardless of their starting position in life. We look out into the future, and we see something that might be. Our dreams energize us and make our hearts leap with the possibility that our lives might be more than they are at present. We might be more, do more, have more, and accomplish more.

Great people throughout human history have been great dreamers. Their dreams have annoyed some and motivated others. As a result of dreams, great cities, cultures, kingdoms, and nations have been built. Great people very often dream dreams that result in opportunities for others to accomplish their own dreams—even to the point that millions and millions of people might accomplish their own dreams.

The ability to dream is God-given. When God looked from heaven into the void, He had a dream. He saw something in nothing. He saw the sun, the moon, the stars, and the incredible vastness of the universe taking shape out of nothing.

He saw the earth with its amazing natural formations, seemingly endless varieties of plant life, and astonishing array of beautiful and distinctive animals taking shape out of nothing. He saw all of the laws that would govern the functions of the universe and the living kingdom on earth, even though they had never existed before. He dreamed it all, and then He created it.

And ultimately God dreamed a dream of mankind. He said, "Let Us make man in Our image"(Gen. 1:26). He molded the clay and formed a being and breathed into it His own Spirit. He put a piece of Himself into each of us, including the desire and capacity to dream.

Many people, however, have lost sight of their dreams, or they have failed to cultivate their ability to dream. Others truly have lost hope for their future, believing that their best days are behind them or that they are destined to live an entire life without having any dream fulfilled. If you fall into either of these categories, I encourage you to rekindle your ability to dream!

Let me give you two overriding principles regarding your dreams:

1. *Dreams usually come to you in pieces.* At one point in your life you may have dreamed one dream, and then later in life you realized that your dream had changed—perhaps only a little, perhaps a lot. Perhaps the initial dream remains intact, but it has expanded or developed to the point that it has several facets. I suggest you revisit your childhood dreams for your life. What did you once hope for yourself? Are those dreams still valid? In what ways? In what ways do your current dreams differ? Can you see ways in which today's dreams are similar to your childhood dreams?

Most of us have bits of dreams. A major challenge that each of us faces is discovering just how these bits of dreams might come together. All genuine dreams are ultimately related and comprise a whole.

2. *Dreams are intuitive.* Dreams are related at a very deep emotional, psychological, and spiritual level to the person you truly are and have strong potential for becoming.

You can achieve any dream that you dream consistently over time, in some fashion, to some degree, at some point, and perhaps after development of specific talents and skills. We rarely dream dreams that are totally beyond our intuitive desire or ability to accomplish them.

Please note that I don't consider temporary, fleeting whims to be dreams. At some point, virtually every person I know has imagined himself flying without a plane! That's a whim. Others dream they become the leader of the entire world, live on Jupiter, or marry a rich foreign king. More whims. Such whims quickly pass when a person is confronted by unchangeable facts. We come quickly to an intuitive and rational conclusion that such whims aren't "doable."

Many people imagine themselves as movie stars, but for most people, that is a whim that lasts only days or perhaps a few weeks at most. For others, however, a dream to act on stage or in movies is truly and genuinely a dream. It is a dream they pursue with their whole hearts, even if it means working long hours without pay.

GENUINE DREAM OR PASSING WHIM?

How can you tell if your dream is a genuine dream or a passing whim? Here are my criteria:

1. *Genuine dreams last over time.* They deepen and grow, perhaps with some variation. They remain in your heart.

2. *Genuine dreams do not negate natural and physical laws* (such as gravity, the laws of physics, and so forth). Neither do they negate the validity or consequences of man-made laws and God-ordained commandments.

3. *Genuine dreams are related to talents and behaviors, not merely to "states of being" you hope to achieve.* To become famous, to be a star, to become rich, to be happy—these are "states of being." To perform onstage or in movies, to work as an elected government official, to own a successful business, to become president of an established company, to work as a newscaster, to become a parent—these are actions that are linked to talents, skills, or behaviors.

Take a moment to reflect upon some of your childhood dreams. Were they whims, fantasies, or pie-in-the-sky hopes, or were they genuine dreams born out of your intuition and a reflection of what you desire most to do in life?

How do these genuine dreams of your childhood relate to who you are and what you do today? How do they relate to the current dreams you might identify?

Dreams Beg to Be Turned into Plans

It isn't enough to know what you'd like to be and do. Dreams accomplish nothing, not even character building. A dream must move beyond the wishful thinking stage to become a set of goals and working plans. The dream of "being a better person" is too vague. How do you define that? What does it mean in practical, definable terms? Does it mean you want to be more honest, work harder, pray more, spend more time with family members, volunteer more, give more, or have more patience?

As your dreams take form, ask even more questions. What does it mean to be more honest? To work harder? To pray more? To spend more time with your family? To volunteer? To give? To have more patience? How much work or prayer or time is enough? In which areas of your life do honesty and patience need to be applied?

Dreams beg to be turned into activity. And that activity must always be rooted in your talents.

Dreams may frame your potential, but your talents are the substance of your potential.

Do We Ever Reach Our Full Potential?

Do we ever realize our full potential? I doubt it. As stated earlier, I believe very strongly that potential is revealed to us as we act on the gifts we have been given. The measure of your greatness in life is in direct proportion to the percentage of your potential that you actualize. If you keep doing what you have been gifted to do—using your gifts for the benefit of others and for a cause greater than yourself—you will grow as a person. And the more you grow, the more potential you will see on the horizon of your life. You may not grow in position and power, but you can grow your potential.

I described potential earlier as being like the horizon—we never reach the edge of the horizon. Potential is also like a river. Have you ever been on a float trip down a river—perhaps on a raft or in a canoe or kayak? Round one bend of the river, and the river continues. Make your way through one set of rapids, and the river very often turns into calm water that requires an active paddle. Make your way through the calm waters and around the next bend, and you may face another set of rapids. The river unfolds as you take the journey. Rarely do you see the whole of it, and never can you know in advance every turn, obstacle, challenge, thrill, scene of beauty, or interesting phenomenon you are going to face.

Potential unfolds in much the same manner. It always lies ahead of us, always compels us forward.

If we saw our full potential at the outset of life's journey, we likely would be so overwhelmed by it that we would be paralyzed, and if not paralyzed, we likely would become so arrogant that our pride would become a major stumbling block to us.

I have seen this happen in the lives of some of the people to whom I have offered organizational consulting when they receive an initial glimpse of their potential. I have met some who told me they were called to accomplish a certain mission. Certainly I don't argue with a calling. As far as I am concerned, we are all called and challenged to accomplish some mission on this earth. Some people, however, become arrogant in their calling to the point of assuming *they* are called—but nobody else is called. The result has been that they have manipulated, ridiculed, or discounted every other person with a similar calling. They have also tended to manipulate, ridicule, and discount those they hire to work for them, thinking that their employees have a "servant" calling that is not of equal value to their own. Essentially they take the attitude, "I am called. I am special. You aren't. My potential is vast. Your potential is far less." That's an unfortunate posture to take, and it many times results in a personal failure.

This attitude is not limited to those who feel a special calling in life. It is sometimes true for those who feel that they have been blessed with a large inheritance, those who feel that they have been uniquely gifted to establish a large company, and those who feel that they are personally gifted to be "superstars" in their fields.

In sharp contrast, there are others who catch a glimpse of what they might become and do with God's help, and they cower in fear at the prospect. They put obstacles in their own path to assure their failure. They refuse to get wise counsel and take action. They would rather do nothing than risk failure, rejection, criticism, ridicule, or dashed hopes. They live in a suspended state of knowing that they are capable of being and doing more, yet not acting. They wind up disillusioned, frustrated, and discouraged by their own cowardice.

Again, this is not only true of those who feel that they are uniquely gifted. It is also true of many who recognize that they are talented in a specific field. They do nothing to develop their talents and tend to blame others for their failure to acquire the education or mentoring they believe they need. They fail to practice. When given opportunities to use their talents—or to perform—they back away with excuses. They live in fear of their ability, and they end up feeling extremely unfulfilled at life's end.

God's plan is "revealed" potential. Bit by bit, *as we use our gifts,* it is revealed to us what more we might become and do. Not the whole picture but a bigger picture is revealed. If we do it right, we move from height to height, from one level to the next, one rung of the ladder at a time.

You Can Learn to Be Great

I feel certain you have heard someone say, "That person is a born leader," or "That person has been great all his life." Most, if not all, leadership classes I have attended have taught that great leaders are born, not made.

Yet I don't believe that is true. I do believe that we are all born with a different starting point on a path toward personal greatness. Every person has the potential for personal greatness. Every person has the potential to exert influence and to lead. The world cannot simply be divided into leaders and followers. As a matter of fact, good leaders are also good followers!

I cannot make the statement too often: *the foremost person you will ever lead in your life is yourself.*

You make the decisions that determine your behavior.

You make the decisions that determine your associations, your affiliations, your relationships, and your schedule.

You make the choices about how, when, and in what ways you will reflect your values, morals, and ethical framework.

You hold the values that shape your choices.

You are the leader of *you*.

I am 100 percent positively and adamantly convinced that all genuine leadership begins at the personal level. The number-one person you need to learn to lead is yourself.

Only you can lead yourself, and you *must* choose to lead yourself if you are going to pursue your potential and achieve personal greatness! If you never become a leader of anyone else, leadership of yourself is sufficient. It is the recognition that you are responsible for leading yourself, and the pursuit of the qualities, traits, values, and acts of service associated with such personal leadership that will result in your achieving personal greatness.

LEAD OR BE LED

Either you lead your own life, or you are led by someone else.

Through the years, I have been to numerous seminars and conferences on leadership. Several years ago, however, I reached the point where I said to myself, "I need to learn how to lead my own life and not be led by somebody or something else." I embarked on a quest to learn how to lead my life.

Many people I encounter in my business of consulting are led by others, or they are driven by the strength of their own personalities and a deep desire for power, fame, wealth or accomplishment. Thankfully, many are also committed openly to being led by the values and principles they most strongly claim to be true and worthy.

Our values and principles are like the rudder on a ship. They can give direction to what we do and lead us safely and productively into ports of our choosing. When values and principles are ignored—or perhaps suppressed by our other personality-based drives for external accomplishment—the forward motion of our personal ship is subject to whatever happens. It's like a ship being guided by the random pattern of wind and wave currents. A person might just as easily enter a safe port as dash against perilous rocks.

The great challenge, therefore, is not the challenge of achieving leadership that can be measured in external trappings of power and control, numbers and status, position and personality. Rather, the challenge before us is the challenge of unlocking the leader within. It is the challenge of pursuing personal greatness and inner convictions that inspire and motivate others. It is the challenge of unlocking our potential, exercising it through positive influence, and linking the "being" and "doing" aspects of our lives into a solid, dynamic whole.

Just as I once had to change my grip in handling a golf club, I also had to change my thinking about greatness and leadership. I had to say no to the traditional claims and embark on a path to lead rather than be led.

What about you? Are you willing to change your idea about who can become a leader, and more important, are you willing to embrace the possibility that you can become great?

REEVALUATING THE VOICES THAT TRY TO LEAD YOU

To choose to lead yourself is an intentional choice. It is a choice most people don't make. Rather, they allow themselves to be led by voices from their past, or by voices that seem to call to them from the external world. These voices frame a person's thinking. They provide a very subtle, ever-present perspective that manifests itself in decisions and choices made every day.

1. Voices from the Past

Some follow voices from the past—words uttered by parents, grandparents, teachers, and other authority figures from their childhood and teenage years. They are still listening to what others said they could do, would do, or should do, or what others said they would never be able to do.

I know an immensely talented man who was told throughout his childhood and teenage years, "You are never going to amount to anything. I'm always going to have to support you." As far as I am concerned, this man's father—a talented, hardworking, and highly successful millionaire—was guilty of emotional child abuse!

Indeed, his son became an adult who achieved *moments* of greatness, but he never achieved a *life* of personal greatness because he still heard and heeded the voice of his father. Repeatedly, just when he was on the brink of establishing consistency, stability, and steadfastness in any area of personal virtue or success, he did something dramatic to dismantle, deconstruct, or destroy his achievement and integrity. He never truly believed he could amount to anything, and he continually proved himself—and his father—right.

On the other hand, I know people whose parents told them what I have told my children repeatedly, "You can do anything you set your mind and talents to do. You can achieve any dream that God has placed in your heart. You can be anything you seek to be if you believe it." People who grow up with that continual positive voice of affirmation are much more likely to achieve personal greatness, and to have a consistency and a surefootedness about their walk through life. They exude confidence and optimism that keep them steady and also keep them moving toward their goals.

What voice from the past is influencing your present life?

2. Voices from the Present

Some follow voices from their present—supervisors at work, religious leaders, therapists (who take many forms, from psychologists to next-door neighbors to "answer man" gurus on their favorite television talk shows), spouses, and others generally in authority positions. One way to tell if you are under the influence of such voices from the present is to monitor your language. Are you continually quoting others or referencing others, using phrases such as, "As Dr. So-and-So said," or "As Mr. Such-and-Such always says," or "As Rev. Prime-Time says"?

What voices from the present are leading your life? Are they voices that are speaking truth to you? Are they voices of people with whom you have a personal relationship? Are they voices you are trusting more than you trust your own voice?

3. Voices of Things, Not People

Still others hear and follow the voices of things, status, or fame that seem to call to them continually. They allow themselves to be led by what they desire to acquire or obtain. They live in pursuit of things they hope to achieve or own or accomplish—if they are lucky, if time permits, or "if things work out."

What is the last thing you think about before you fall asleep? What is the first thing you think about when you awaken?

If it is a negative experience—from a disease to an accident to an unpleasant potential encounter—you very likely are listening to the voice of fear.

If it's something substantive that you are seeking to consume, use, or experience physically, you may be listening to a voice of addiction.

If it's a desire for a particular possession, position of prominence, or promotion to greater status, you may be listening to a voice of greed, or of lust for power or fame.

What voices call to you in the hours when you are alone?

4. Voices of Immediate Need

Still others hear and follow the voices of emotions and circumstances. They allow their lives to be dictated by external needs or problems. They move from emotion to emotion, circumstance to circumstance, situation to situation, and sometimes crisis to crisis, making decisions on the basis of resolving the immediate need as quickly and painlessly as possible. They tend to be focused on acquiring the bare essentials for life.

For these people, life is led by something on the outside instead of something on the inside.

WHOSE LIFE ARE YOU LEADING?

Ask yourself today: *Whose life am I leading?*

Very few people follow their voices from within and pursue dreams that are an extension of who they are on the inside. Those who choose to pursue personal greatness recognize they have been shaped by voices from the past and are influenced by voices from the present, but they also have made a concerted effort to know their own voices and to listen to the voice of God. They have made the choice to listen first to themselves and to give the greatest weight to their own beliefs, values, and opinions.

KEY QUESTIONS TO ASK

Ask yourself these important questions about possible influences on your choices, decisions, and behavior:

- *Did others teach me the truth? Are others telling me the truth now?*

- *Did the person who was influencing my life have any motive other than what was best for me?*

- *Was there any attempt to manipulate me for their own purposes and self-gratification?*

- *Who are the great influencers in my life today? What fruit have they produced in their own lives?*

The person who leads himself has sifted through, and continues to sift through, thousands of messages about who he is and what he should do in his life. He has determined what he holds to be true. The person who has firmly grasped the reins of self-leadership has truly come to know himself from the inside out—rather than follow the norm of responding to life from the outside in.

A number of years ago I found myself at a crossroads, about to embark on a new career, when I came to the startling conclusion that I really didn't know where I was going in my life. The truth was, I really didn't know who I was, and therefore, I couldn't possibly know where I was going.

Rather than allow myself to become preoccupied with external factors—how much money I needed to pay my bills, the opportunities that presented themselves, the jobs that were offered—I took time to take a long, hard look at myself.

Have you ever paused to do that—not a pause in a sense of a momentary reflection, but a pause in the sense of allowing your life to come to a full stop?

THE GREAT VALUE OF SELF-REFLECTION

There are times when it is good for a person to drop all memberships and commitments and withdraw from extraneous activity to conduct some deep soul-searching.

I have a friend named Ben. He's a wonderful person, he has a great family, and I have no doubt that if you met him today, you'd love him.

Ben has been haunted for years, however, with the fact that he has never figured out his purpose in life. He has never identified his talents. Oh, he may be able to give you a general idea, but he has never stopped to reflect on what he truly is good at doing innately and naturally. He has never reflected on his intelligence, spiritual gifts, core values, or deep desires. He can tell you in a general way what he believes and how he wants to behave, but he has no real understanding of how his beliefs relate to his service to others.

Ben is now in his midforties, and he's frustrated. He has spent nearly twenty years moving from one thing to the next to the next to the next. Every time a greater opportunity or a better situation presented itself, Ben jumped at it. He has lived the past two decades answering the question *What should I do next?* rather than ask the question of himself, *Why do I do what I do?* He has looked to wiser, more experienced, more successful people to tell him what he should do rather than determine from within his soul what direction he should take in his life.

Just recently Ben's wife said to him, "I'm tired of going from one thing to the next. The kids are tired of moving from one city to the next. Please figure out what you want out of life and focus on it." Ben is trying to do as she has asked. He has admitted to himself, and to me as his friend, that he's tired of moving frequently—not just moving to new cities but to new jobs and new interests. But he doesn't know where to start in evaluating his inner self.

He said to me, "Thinking about yourself is tough. It's easier to think about how to get a problem solved or a task done or to make a sale."

My response was this: "Thinking about your life may be the toughest thing you'll ever do, but in the end—if you truly think through who you are and come to some conclusions about what you want to be, what you want to contribute to life, and what character traits you want to embody—you will come to some decisions that will give you the rewarding, stable life both you and your family desire."

I believe that with all my heart.

A friend of mine named David, at age twenty, got down on his knees and asked, "God, why am I here?" He went to India, spent six months in missionary service there, and returned home with a clear directive that he believes came from God. He can tell you today in very clear terms, "This is why I exist." He knows his core beliefs, his talents, his goals, and his purpose for living. He has hooked up his life to a cause greater than himself. He is a servant to all those around him.

Through the years David has experienced more personal adversity than just about any person I know. But through it all, he has been able to bounce back again and again and again. Why? I believe his success is due largely to the fact that he knows who he is, why he exists, and to what he is committed. He lives out of a purpose to serve and help others succeed. It is so strong that you can feel it just by standing next to him!

Is David more talented than Ben? No. Does he have a more dynamic personality? No. A more stable family background or early childhood? No. Does he have a more understanding spouse or better friends? No.

What David has that Ben doesn't have is a very clear understanding that

- renewal is possible
- purpose is ongoing
- fear must be conquered
- a person's destiny can be discovered and pursued
- process is more important than events
- principles are greater than personality
- service is the ultimate success
- giving is the key to receiving

David has made rock-solid foundational decisions regarding his life and the character hallmarks he has chosen to embrace and embody. David has chosen to lead his life rather than be led by circumstances, opportunities, or crises.

THE PRIVILEGE OF SELF-LEADERSHIP

One of the greatest freedoms our nation affords us is the privilege of self-leadership.

Our government does not dictate what kind of schooling you will receive, where you will receive it, or how much of it you can have. In many countries around the world, educational paths are dictated by governments. Not in our nation. You can pursue school, or some form of continuing education, as long as you desire, as much as you desire, in virtually any area of your interest. You can lead your own life in the area of self-improvement.

Our government does not dictate what kind of church you should attend or prohibit you from attending the church of your choice. That's not true in many nations that adhere to a state religion and that actively punish—in some cases, to the point of death—any person who does not participate in or give lip service to the prevailing religion. In our country you can lead your own life in the area of spiritual development.

Our government does not dictate to you how many children you can have or whether you must produce children in order to be afforded certain privileges in society. That's not true in some nations, including the nation on this earth that has one-sixth of the world's population. But in our country you can lead your own life when it comes to the size of your family.

Neither does our government—or culture—dictate the person you will marry. That's not true in many cultures. In our nation, you can lead your own love life.

Our government does not dictate where you may live, how you may travel, what kind of job you must have, how much work you must produce, how much money you must earn (or cannot earn), or how you use your leisure time. There are no governmental restrictions on what you choose to watch on television or see in theaters, or the type of music you choose to listen to on radio stations. Furthermore, there are no stipulations on where you can go for recreation or vacation, which clubs you may choose to join, or how you may choose to spend a day off. That's not true in many nations. You have the opportunity to lead your own life when it comes to making choices about how you spend your time, money, and energy. You can lead your own life when it comes to output and input.

These are tremendous areas for leadership.

Don't take these privileges lightly.

EVEN IF YOU DON'T FEEL LIKE A LEADER . . .

My wife, Joy, said to me one day, "I don't feel a lot of purpose for my life." At the time, our last child was preparing to leave home for college. My wife had left her career to be a stay-at-home wife and mother, and after twenty years of fulfilling that role as well or better than any person I have ever met, she was feeling a little empty. She said, "You are writing about achieving personal greatness and leadership and how every person can be a leader—I don't feel at all like I am great."

This was my response to Joy: "You may not see yourself as great, but I can tell you three people who think you are—your husband, your son, and your daughter. Not only do the three of us see you as a person who has exercised her potential, exerted tremendously positive influence, and been a role model worthy of emulation, but there are countless people you don't even know who have witnessed your life as a wife and mother and who have said to themselves, 'I want to be more like Joy.' Not only that, but there are going to be people who are told about you and will begin to think, *I'd like to be a person like that.*" Some of those doing the telling are likely to be our children who, in following Joy's leadership, will demonstrate some of the same excellent values and character qualities that she demonstrated as their mother. I have no doubt about it.

You may not think today that you are having any positive influence on others or that you are moving into personal greatness as a leader. Chances are, you haven't fully recognized that you are a leader in certain areas and to certain people. What's required is that you change your thinking.

Make the choice to lead yourself and to do what's necessary to grow in self-leadership.

Do the often difficult but always beneficial work of self-reflection and self-discovery as you analyze who and what has been leading your life.

Act on the privilege to determine what kind of leader you will be of yourself.

Begin to see yourself as a leader—even if you never have

seen yourself as a leader, and even if you don't believe any-body else sees you as a leader.

Again I say to you, you must change your thinking and choose to lead your own life. You are the leader of you!

WHERE AND HOW DO YOU BEGIN?

How do you open the door that leads you to a pathway of developing personal greatness and leadership?

You begin first by understanding the seven principles that guide you on the path toward achieving personal greatness. By *guide* I do not mean "dictate" or "take you by the hand and compel you to follow." Rather, these principles keep you focused toward greatness. They are like the curbs on the side of a street. They keep you from wandering off into the ditches of discouragement or despair. They also keep you on the road, moving toward your goals rather than stopping at a rest area or getting off the road and onto a tangential detour that can waste time, energy, and resources.

These guiding principles are not only true for all people at all times and in all places and all cultures, but they are truths that you need to accept and internalize in such a way that they become your perspective, your worldview, your way of seeing your life. In that way, they guide your choices and your decisions—your attitudes, your words, your feel-ings, your behaviors. In that way, they guide you toward achieving personal greatness.

THE 7 GUIDING PRINCIPLES OF UNLOCKING YOUR POTENTIAL

Embracing Essential Truths

All of us are guided by principles that we hold to frame truth. They give us a perspective on life, a foundation for responding to various choices and decisions. The stronger our belief in a principle, the more likely that principle is to motivate us to act.

I strongly believe there are seven principles that are absolutely essential for you to embrace. Unless you embrace these principles fully, you are unlikely to pursue personal greatness and even less likely to achieve it.

As you read through these guiding principles, I encourage you to ask yourself repeatedly: *Do I really believe this? Do I believe it for myself? In other words, do I believe this principle applies to me? How strongly do I believe this? Am I willing to act on my belief?*

YOU ARE BORN WITH GOD-GIVEN POTENTIAL

EVERY PERSON IS BORN WITH SOME TALENT. NOT ALL talents are the same, and not all talents are distributed equally.

Most of us are familiar with this line from the Declaration of Independence: "We hold these Truths to be self-evident, that all Men are created equal." Equal at what? The Declaration defines equality in fairly narrow terms: "that they are endowed by their Creator with certain unalienable Rights, that among these are Life, Liberty, and the Pursuit of Happiness." We may have an equal legal right in our nation to life, freedom, and the *pursuit* of happiness. The reality is also this: not all people are created equal when it comes to *potential*—or to the distribution of talents, skills, abilities, dreams, desires, or intelligence.

Some people have more talents than others. Some people are intellectually brighter, more athletic, more musical, more perceptive, more artistic, more empathetic, more gifted in dealing with words, more gifted in dealing with numbers, and so forth. But each person is born with some talent.

Furthermore, talents and abilities seem to be fairly random in their distribution. While there are some outstanding examples of "like father, like son" or "like mother, like daughter," the greater truth appears to be that talents and natural gifts do not flow through family lines. Unparalleled musicians have produced tone-deaf children; outstanding entrepreneurs often have children with absolutely no propensity for or interest in business; artists bear children who turn out to be scientists; genius talent often emerges from parents who are "just average."

We cannot predetermine the talents of our children, just as we had no say in the talents we were given at our birth. We had no say in whether we would be a five-talent, two-talent, or one-talent person.

You may say, "It isn't fair." So be it. It isn't ours to determine what's fair.

The good news, however, is twofold. Each of us is born with some talent and, therefore, some potential. Each of us is given some opportunity to develop that talent. Each of us has some opportunity to influence others.

What we receive at birth is our starting point in life, not the ending point. We have the opportunity to take what we are given at birth and work with it.

This guiding principle is important for you to embrace for two main reasons:

First, your potential is all about you. There's a popular phrase in our American culture today: "It's all about you." Well, when it comes to potential, it *is* all about you. There's value in focusing on what talents and abilities you have been given from birth. There's no value in comparing what you have been given with what someone else has been given.

If you get into the comparison game, you will always be disappointed. You'll always be able to find somebody who can do a task better, faster, or with greater ease. You'll always find somebody who can run faster, jump higher, lift heavier weights, hit the ball farther, or score more points. You'll always find somebody who wins more, earns more, or has more. There's no end to the comparison. And there's no joy in comparison. The end result of comparison is always personal discouragement, and discouragement keeps a person from pursuing what is possible. Anytime the focus is on what *isn't*—or any other negative, for that matter—the result is a stifling of energy or a decrease in motivation to pursue a goal.

Refuse to play the comparison game. Focus instead on what you have, and what you can do.

Second, there are those who never take the first step toward personal greatness because they do not believe they have any talent or ability. Or they may not go to that extreme, saying instead, "I have so little talent," or "I have no ability to do anything others might value."

Anytime you undervalue your potential, you decrease your worth in your eyes. Always keep in mind that the degree to which you value your ability is the degree to which others will value your ability.

We all know people who think of themselves more highly than they ought. Nobody likes to be around a bragging, pompous, self-absorbed, proud person. On the other hand, we also know people who think more lowly of themselves than they ought. And the truth about these people is this: nobody wants to be around a falsely humble, doormat-projecting, self-deprecating person who always seems to be begging for compliments or praise.

The person who proclaims, "I can do all things better than anybody," seems to be asking for truth serum. The person who says, "I can't do anything," seems to be asking to be ignored or coddled.

Own up to the fact that you have potential. Take the attitude: "I have some ability, and I'd like to see what I might be able to do in life." With that attitude you will be willing to pursue, and continue to pursue, personal greatness. Other people will be eager to help you when you have that attitude.

Say with boldness today: "I am a person with God-given talent and potential!"

You Must Accept the Challenge of Discovering Your Talents and Abilities

You were not born with an instruction manual tied to your wrist. You face the challenge of finding out what you are good at doing, what you choose to value, and what you choose to do with the talents you have.

Very few of us have a major experience of revelation in which we suddenly know precisely what we are gifted to do or how we should apply our talents to a particular endeavor, career, or cause. That's by design! Life is a process of discovery, not a prescription to be followed.

It isn't easy to discern the skills at which we may be talented or what character traits we should develop. Nevertheless, we apply ourselves to developing our character and turning our talents into skills.

Why is it necessary to embrace this guiding principle? Because if you are waiting for your talents to emerge, without any discovery effort on your part, you may spend your entire lifetime on the sidelines rather than jumping in and actively exploring your potential and your depths and heights of personal greatness.

Don't expect or allow other people to define what you are good at doing. Find out for yourself.

Don't expect or allow other people to set your goals or identify your dreams. Set your own goals and identify your own dreams.

Discover *yourself*—for yourself, by yourself.

Say boldly today: "I can and will discover my talents and pursue my potential!"

YOU MUST ACCEPT RESPONSIBILITY FOR DEVELOPING YOUR TALENTS

THE CHALLENGE LIES BEFORE YOU: TAKE OWNERSHIP of your talents and assume responsibility for their development and use.

Do you value yourself enough to want to become and to do all that you are capable of becoming and doing? Do you want to achieve all you can achieve, give all you can give, and positively influence others to the full extent that you can?

Talents nearly always need to be developed into skills. For example, you may have great athletic ability, but you still have to learn the game. You may have great musical ability—an excellent voice, sense of rhythm, and so forth—but you still have to learn to sing or to play an instrument. And if you want to play in an orchestra or marching band, you are going to have to learn to read music.

You may have an innate propensity and desire to serve other people, but if you channel that desire into preparing food for other people, you are going to need to develop the skills associated with cooking. If you desire to serve people in the medical profession, you are going to have to learn the skills associated with nursing or doctoring.

The more you develop a talent, turning it into an observable, measurable, definable set of skills, the more you are likely to discover related talents. Building on the examples in the previous paragraph—if you have athletic ability that you have turned into a skill at baseball, you may discover in the course of developing this ability that you have related abilities in coaching or providing commentary on baseball games. If you have musical ability and develop skills as a musician, you may discover that you also have the ability to teach music skills to others, critique musical performances, or compose or arrange music.

No talent is ever fully developed in a person's lifetime—there's always more that can be learned, explored, or honed to perfection. No matter how much a person knows or can do, there's always more to learn and more to do.

The good news, however, is that the more you exercise your talents and develop your skills, the greater enjoyment and satisfaction you are likely to experience in the use of your talents. The better a person plays golf, the more that person is likely to enjoy playing golf. The better a pianist can play the piano, the more that musician is likely to enjoy playing the piano. The more competent a person is at cooking or nursing, the more that person is likely to feel personal satisfaction at serving a gourmet meal or saving a patient's life.

Choose to develop your talents, and continue to develop them. Choose to see just how good you can become at doing the thing you are good at doing and enjoy doing most!

Why is it important to embrace this guiding principle

fully? Because the person who never turns talents into skills is a person about whom others say, "He had so much ability. He just never *did* anything with it."

We all know people like that—those who have fine minds, but don't study, obtain no degrees, never focus on any areas of interest, make no contributions. There is a fine voice, but no practice, no performance, no sharing of the gift with others. Some may have green thumbs, but there is no planting, no cultivating, no garden, no produce, no fruitfulness.

Don't rely on others to nag you into the training, education, practice, application, rehearsal, or goal setting required for turning a talent into a skill. Motivate yourself to build something on the foundation you have been given.

Say boldly today: "I can and will develop all my talents and abilities to a level of excellence!"

You Should Pursue Potential with a Sense of Urgency

Do you feel an urgency about developing your talents? Or do you have a lackadaisical, I'll-get-around-to-it-eventually attitude about turning your innate abilities into skills? Waste no time. Act on what you know to do.

Today is the day you have been given. Do something with it.

None of us are given full vision into the total outcome or the big picture of our lives. Rather, we are given glimpses of what we might become, might do, might have, or might accomplish if we apply ourselves to the attainment of the destiny we see before us. The caveat always seems to be there: *if* we take action. Nothing about our ultimate success is handed to us on a silver platter.

Do you have a sense of urgency about identifying your talents, developing and improving skills related to your talents, increasing your knowledge, and deepening your relationships with other people and with God? Do you have a sense of urgency about working, growing, changing, improving, developing, and maturing?

You must embrace this guiding principle fully for one main reason: if you don't take action today, you aren't likely to take action tomorrow or any other day in the future. You may live with great hope and anticipation and expectation, but you will never live in the reality of accomplishment and achievement.

Say boldly today: "I will act *now* to take the next step in turning my talents into skills, and the next step in using my skills to influence others positively."

You Must Face
Down the Fear of Failure

Refuse to give in to fear—it will only hold you back.

Fear is probably the most damaging of all emotions when it comes to the pursuit of your potential. If you live in fear of what others will do or say, you aren't going to take the risks necessary to grow and develop as a person. If you fear failure, you aren't going to take a training course to improve your skills. If you fear rejection, you aren't going to apply for a promotion. If you fear that a financial loss will be beyond your ability to recover from it, you aren't going to make any less-than-a-sure-deal financial investments.

How many people do you know who are blaming others for their lack of success? At the root of blaming others is generally fear. It is very easy for a person who fears failure to say to himself and others, "I didn't take action because somebody else stood in my way or got there before I did."

Ask yourself today, *What am I afraid of?* Get to the heart of the reason that you haven't pursued, aren't pursuing, or don't plan to pursue and develop your talents and potential.

"I'm not afraid," you may be saying. "I just don't want to make the effort."

Are you lazy?

Probably not.

I frequently encounter people who say they have no energy, inclination, or desire to pursue their talents or develop their skills, but they seem to have amazing energy when it is time to pursue their hobbies or favorite sports. At issue is probably the way they have defined talents and potential.

Talents aren't related only to careers, work, or jobs that provide income. Talents encompass the whole of a person's life. And the ideal is probably this: choose to work and make money in the area in which you are talented, even if that seems like a hobby, leisure-time activity, or recreational sport!

Are you afraid to quit a paying job to pursue what you love to do but have never yet earned a dime doing? Face up to that fear.

What would you do today if you knew with certainty you would succeed at it, love doing it, and find fulfillment in it?

That's the very thing you should be pursuing in some way, to some degree. Face up to the fear that's holding you back.

Say boldly today: "I will not fear failure—I will pursue my talents and potential with faith, hope, energy, and optimism."

You Must Use Your Talents or Lose Them

In plain language: if you don't do it, somebody else will.

How many times have you said to yourself, *Wow—I had that idea. I had the talent to do that. I had the ability to accomplish that. I could have won that race, been given that award, achieved that promotion?* But because you didn't do anything with the idea, somebody else invented the product, established the procedure, got the part, started the company, created the design, discovered the solution, implemented the strategy, or published the manuscript.

The prize goes to the person who trains for and runs the race. If you don't train and you don't run, you won't win the prize. It's as simple as that.

In all likelihood, there's a better job today that you could be doing, but you aren't doing it because you didn't pursue it and somebody else now has it.

There's likely a greater ministry role or function that you could be doing, but you aren't because you didn't step out in faith when you should have. But somebody else did, and now he is doing it and will receive the eternal reward for having done it.

There's an opportunity that could have yielded a great reward to you, but you didn't prepare for it or pursue it, and as a result, another person grabbed the brass ring.

There's an area of success waiting for you today in every area of your life. If you don't move into it, somebody else will.

Good ideas don't die. They just pop into somebody else's head.

WHY DON'T WE ACT?

A major constraint that keeps someone from acting on an idea, pursuing a talent, or developing a skill is the belief that only a very limited number of people can or will succeed in life. Many people believe that only a particular segment of society, a particular organization, or a select group of people have the corner on success. Not only that, but people who hold to this belief tend to believe that those who are successful in some way keep them out of the success arena or refuse to give them a chance to participate in ventures that yield success. The result is that they feel put down, excluded, impeded, or denied. They attribute their lack of success to somebody else; they never take responsibility for their failure to exert effort or act on a wise decision or creative idea.

Let me assure you, you will never truly develop your talents if you are preoccupied with other people and what they have, what they do, what they say, or who they are. You will never truly move into your potential as long as you are preoccupied with the obstacles that you believe are going to limit you, hold you back, or keep you down. You won't succeed if you are bound up with jealousy over what another person has. As long as your focus is on what others have—and what you don't have but want—you are going to be bitter, angry, and resentful. In turn, you are going to be less energetic, less creative, less willing to work alongside others as a team player, and less productive or efficient as you work for others in authority over you.

When you are jealous of another person or are judgmental of his character, you rarely impact his life for good, and you are the one who loses. You are the one who appears petty, mean-spirited, and motivated by negativity. You are the one who, in your jealousy, does not pursue what is *rightfully yours* because you are too preoccupied with what is *rightfully someone else's*.

Choose to respect those for whom you work and with whom you associate. Value what others do and the ways in which they contribute to your life. Refuse to give in to envy or to develop a judgmental spirit. Doing so will only hold you back.

THE SHRINKING OF POTENTIAL

In addition to your losing out because you don't take action on your ideas, insights, or interests, you are subject to this general law of the universe: if you don't use it, you lose it.

We all know that to be true with our physical muscles. Lack of use results in atrophy—a withering away into weakness and inability. The principle is also true for our mental abilities. If we stop exercising the mind by challenging it in new ways—from solving puzzles to learning new information to engaging in thought-compelling conversations and discussions—we lose mental acuity. The same is true for talents. Even the most accomplished musicians still practice scales, the most accomplished golfers still go out for practice rounds, and the best football teams still spend the week before the Super Bowl running drills.

And that isn't all. If you fail to pursue your potential, you will lose sight of your potential, and you never will develop it to its fullest.

If you see yourself as a failure, you will make no effort to succeed.

If you see yourself as stupid, you will make no effort to learn.

If you see yourself as unlovable, you will make no effort to develop loving friendships.

If you see yourself as unforgivable, you will make no confession of sin; therefore, you will receive no forgiveness of sin.

In the end, if you see yourself as having no potential, you will see yourself as a "zero"—a failure, a have-nothing, do-nothing, am-nothing person. And the end result is that you truly will have failed. You truly will have nothing and will be without accomplishments. You will have no self-esteem or self-worth. You will die inside, even as your future crumbles around you.

Don't let that happen to you!

Don't delay!

The longer you fail to use a talent, the weaker the talent becomes. Writers who want to remain good writers continue to write. The same is true for artists of all kinds. Painters continue to put brush to canvas; sculptors continue to sculpt; designers continue to design. Top executives continue to attend seminars and listen to consultants to stay ahead of the curve in their business field. Cooks continue to experiment with new recipes. Surgeons continue to attend conferences and professional meetings to learn the latest techniques and become acquainted with the newest inventions. Professional athletes keep practicing.

Don't allow your talents to dissipate. Use them.

Don't allow your ideas to gather dust in the dark recesses of a file cabinet. Develop them.

Don't allow your interests to remain daydreams. Act on them!

The ultimate reason to embrace this principle fully is this: self-motivation. Remind yourself often that if you don't do it or act on it to your benefit, somebody else likely will act on it to his benefit. If you don't use the talents you have, you'll lose them. They will waste away into nothing.

Say with boldness today and frequently, "I must use my talents and exercise my skills!"

FULFILLING YOUR POTENTIAL IS A CHARACTER ISSUE

IT DOESN'T MATTER HOW MUCH MATERIAL WEALTH YOU end up with in life. It doesn't matter how many heirs you leave behind. It doesn't matter how many degrees you earned or awards you were given. What matters at the end of life is that you are in right relationship with your Creator and that you have developed the talents He has given you and developed the character likeness He desires for you to have.

Answer honestly: Are you doing all that you know God created you to do and desires for you to do? Are you fulfilling His purpose for your existence? Are you living the life that He declares will give you the greatest personal satisfaction and fulfillment? Will you be able to stand before your Creator one day and say, "I did everything I knew to do with all that You gave me"?

YOU CANNOT OVERACHIEVE

When you exercise your potential and seek to positively influence others, you *increase* your potential and your opportunities for influence. Potential continues to loom before you throughout your life as long as you are producing out of the past development of the talents you have been given.

The horizon doesn't end; it only expands. Any journey on foot is eventually going to end at the edge of an ocean, and if a boat can be found, the journey extends to the middle of a sea. Then there's nothing but sky, water, and a horizon that is a complete circle around a person—a virtually unending, limitless potential that can be pursued in any number of directions!

So it is, too, with our potential. In the end, we never fulfill our potential. Rather, we move into an understanding that our potential is as vast as God's provision to us. Our potential is as big as our faith, as broad as our hope, as wide as our desire to become all we can become and do all we can do.

You cannot overachieve.

No. The process is one in which you continually grow and expand and develop and pursue. And it is in the pursuit of your potential that your potential expands, grows, and develops in front of you. As your potential grows and you pursue it, you grow. As you grow, your potential unfolds and grows before you.

What an exciting way to live!

And what an absolutely vital concept for you to grasp as you seek to become the leader of your life and to achieve personal greatness.

There are countless examples of two-talent and one-talent people who have surpassed five-talent people because they chose to exercise their potential. If a five-talent person stops pursuing his potential, he will not see that potential grow, and he will not grow himself. Before long, a two-talent person who is continually exercising his potential and growing into an expansion of that potential is going to move past him, receiving even greater rewards, accomplishing even greater things, and developing even finer character. The starting point and the ending point are not the main point. The main point is what you are pursuing, how you are growing, and whether you are moving more and more into the fullness of what God has designed for your life.

EMBRACING FULLY YOUR GREATNESS

I knew deep within my spirit as a little boy, *I am going to be great someday*. My definition of *great* is certainly different from the definition of some people. For me, helping other people to achieve personal greatness is the most rewarding thing I can imagine doing. For me, *great* is a necessary forerunner for *greater* or *greatest*. My joy is to be great—a positive influence, maximizing my talents and skills in pursuit of my potential—and to help others become greater than I am and perhaps even the greatest of all in the areas of their potential and influence.

My great desire is to be the leader of leaders—to point the way by what I say and do overtly, to show the way by the example of my life. I cannot imagine a greater or more fulfilling life purpose.

I don't know what your specific talents and areas of influence may be, but I encourage you to seek personal greatness. I encourage you to want to be great. I encourage you to see yourself as a person of potential, talents, and influence.

Choose to do what you know to do to achieve personal greatness and to unlock the leader within.

Only as you give your best effort to being your best self will you produce the best and most influential work that results in the best success!

The next ten chapters present ten powerful keys that can help you unlock your potential and turn it into positive influence. All of the keys have the principles described in this chapter at their foundation—they require a renewal of the mind.

These keys are not difficult to understand, but they do require diligence and discipline. These keys must be used consistently if they are to be effectual.

These keys involve the most enduring aspects of life.

These keys are decisions that are made with the will and with the heart. At the outset, you may need to remind yourself of these keys often. Over time, they should become your automatic response in all places and in all relationships.

Perhaps the best news of all is that these keys are ones that every person holds in his hand. You can use these keys every day, in every situation of your life, in every relationship, and in every role you play!

The 10 Powerful Keys to Releasing and Developing your Potential

Get Your Cart
Before the Horse

You have probably heard the saying, "Don't get your cart before the horse." Well, I want to tell you that the very first step you must take to achieve personal greatness is to do just that—get your cart before the horse. Let me explain.

Recently I sat down with an associate to have a heart-to-heart talk. Without doubt, this man is one of the most brilliant people I have encountered thus far in my life. He has the ability to conceptualize very complicated business deals, take the most complex set of details and make them appear simple, and produce excellent results. His talents have made him a millionaire many times over.

I asked him during our conversation, "Are you happy?"

He snapped his head around and gave me a rather funny look. "No," he said, "I'm not."

I asked, "Are you content?"

"No, I'm not," he said matter-of-factly.

I asked, "What do you think it would take for you to become happy and content?"

He replied, "Oh, I have a few more things I must get done, and then I will be happy."

I can't tell you how many times I have heard other people say the same thing. I have said it myself, and probably you have too! The reason we say, "There are a few more things I have to do," is that we truly believe, deep down inside, that the *doing* of a few more things will result in an inner state of contentment and joy.

Many people I encounter have a checklist of things they believe they need to do: graduate from college, get married, land a fabulous job, become financially independent, buy a house and boat at the lake, you name it. They are looking for the horse that will pull their carts through life. They think once they get that horse going, they will then be able to relax, kick back, and *be* whatever they want to be.

Others take the approach "When I get all the things I need, then I will be happy and fulfilled." We may not be as quick to admit this belief, but it resides in many people nonetheless. They associate accomplishments and possessions with contentment and joy.

How do we acquire these things we believe we need for happiness? Through *doing*—working, trading, bargaining, negotiating, manipulating, planning, achieving. Again, we are back to *doing* as the precursor to *being*.

Most people I know consciously or subconsciously put *doing* before *being*, but the greater reality is this: our potential is more powerfully released when we put being before doing.

If you can learn to operate from the *being* side of life, then everything you desire will come to you as a result. The things you need will come to you as a result of your pursuing your life purpose, and your life purpose is rooted in your *being*. It is the essence of who you are.

Doing Always Flows from Being

Doing flows from being. In other words, you are the cart, and who you are must come before what you do (the horse).

This may seem to be obvious, but it is not the way many people function on a daily basis. Neither is it the way many people approach their careers, their leadership potential, or the creation of their personal lives.

We construct job résumés based upon what we have done. We plan our schedules to accommodate what we intend to do. We write in our journals or diaries what we have done. We plan vacations on the basis of what we hope to do. We make "to do" lists far more than we make "to be" lists.

We want to know what the stock market has done on a given day. We track projects on the basis of what has been done. We give awards and grant promotions and give raises on the basis of how well something is done.

I certainly am not dismissing the value of doing. We occupy the bulk of our hours on any given day by doing. What I am advocating is that the *being* side of our lives predicates and dictates the *doing* side of our lives far more than we recognize. Only when we intentionally take a long, hard look at who we are do we have a better understanding of what we do and far greater insight into what we truly should do.

To lead from within is to lead from the voice of your

deepest desires, beliefs, and principles. It is to lead from your character and values. It is to lead from the inner substance of faith and an awareness of personal worthiness, purpose, and destiny.

To engage in personal greatness is to say, "I choose to live an intentional life. I choose to make decisions and engage in certain activities and behaviors based upon what I firmly hold as values and guiding principles."

LET YOUR VALUES GUIDE YOU

Your values, taken as a whole, provide an inner guiding light that will serve you all of your adult life.

Values are the beliefs that are deeply fixed within you, from which you intuitively make decisions and pass judgments. When your values are violated, you feel guilty or uncomfortable. When your values and your behavior are in sync, you feel positive and at ease. Taken as a whole, *your values are what you believe.*

WHO DO YOU WANT TO BE?

Most of us think in terms of what we might like to do with our lives. We tend to do something, and if we succeed at it, we do it again and again and again.

In actuality, however, what we do is always preceded by who we are. The real premise at work is this: we are what we believe and how we behave, and out of who we are, we act.

Rather than ask ourselves, *What do I want to do?* we need to ask ourselves, *Who do I want to be?*

In many cases, we desire to be just like the people we would most value having in close association with us. We desire to influence others in a positive way. And we desire to make a lasting impact in a meaningful way on those who are important to us.

What character traits do you value as being the most important? Name your personal top ten. If you have difficulty focusing on your values, I offer you this list:

relational	diligent	commited
full of integrity	honest	purposeful
humorous	vibrant	pursuing potential
balanced	mature	affectionate/loving
flexible	joyful	hardworking
optimistic	creative	communicative
determined	dependable	humble
empathetic	encourager of others	friendly
socially skilled	giving	able to solve problems
family oriented	modest	helpful
appreciative	encouraging	devoted to God

VALUES SHAPE YOUR INFLUENCE

Your values are indicators of the way you approach life's critical dimensions. They predict what you choose, how you make decisions, what attracts your interest, how you respond to challenges, and ultimately how you choose to behave.

How you choose to behave generally can be stated in terms of "I will."

What one statement describes how you deal with your physical health and appearance?

What one statement summarizes the values you hold regarding your emotional well-being?

What one statement summarizes the values you hold regarding your spiritual well-being?

What one statement summarizes how you relate to your family?

What one statement summarizes your values related to nonfamily relationships—friends, coworkers, those above and below you on an organizational chart, members of the church or synagogue to which you belong?

What one statement summarizes your values related to the material world of possessions, including money, financial planning, saving, and investing?

What one statement summarizes the values you hold related to learning?

What one statement summarizes your values regarding leadership and success?

What one statement summarizes your values related to the way in which you handle adversity or failure?

Your answers should resonate in the deepest part of you,

with the affirmation, "Yes! This is the basis from which I usually act. This is a statement of what I really believe, what I truly value."

I have provided a summary of the behavior-related statements I personally hold. I encourage you to take some time to identify and write down your own "I will" statements in eight critical dimensions of life: physical, emotional, spiritual, family, relationships, possessions, learning, and leadership.

Consider the values that your statements reflect. Are these truly the values that lie at the core of your *being*?

1. *Physical*: I will build habits in my life that prolong my life and good health.

2. *Emotional*: I will live with passion, fun, and a zest for life.

3. *Spiritual*: I will pursue my relationship with God and be true to His commandments.

4. *Family*: I will take time to understand my wife and children and help make their dreams come true.

5. *Relationships*: I will build relationships that endure for a lifetime.

6. *Possessions*: I will live within my means, and create financial security and a heritage for my family.

7. *Learning*: I will consistently pursue a lifestyle of learning.

8. *Leadership*: I will follow the three nonnegotiable traits of leadership:
   - I will tell the truth.
   - I will do the right thing.
   - I will produce results.

YOUR VALUES AND YOUR LIFE PURPOSE

The values that you hold are not only a key to understanding your choices and behavior, but they are an integral part of your life purpose. What you value and what you believe to be your purpose in life are always closely connected. For example, if you value creativity, you likely believe you have a creative purpose in life. If you value being a good friend, a vital aspect of your purpose in living is likely to be extending friendship to others. If you value a strong faith in God and building up others, you are likely to have a purpose that relates to extending your faith and ministering to others for the purpose of building them up spiritually.

Can you state the purpose for your life in a single sentence?

A life-purpose statement is drawn from your sense of who you are and why you are on the earth. It should reflect the maximum amount of meaning and purpose you have for your life. It is a statement that flows from your inner reality, your true self.

Think in terms of the whole of who you are:

- What is your overall sense of, your overall conclusion about, your overall insight into yourself?

- In what direction does your life seem to be aimed?

- In what do you find the greatest meaning?

- In what type of life are you likely to find the greatest purpose?

- What value-based lifestyle is likely to give you a sense of well-being and satisfaction?

Your answers to these questions should boil down to and provide one key answer to the question: "Why do you exist?"

What are you on the earth to be and to do?

What gives your life meaning?

Your life-purpose statement is the single most important summary statement you can make about your life. It provides a focus for your life. It is an anchor to which you can return again and again in times of turmoil.

Several years ago, I worked as a consultant in a firm that specialized in corporate management. When the day came that I felt I should leave that firm, one of my colleagues asked me, "Well, what are you going to do? If not this, what?"

I said, "I'm going to build people and build organizations."

I will build people and build organizations is my life-purpose statement. That is why I am on this earth. A builder of people and a builder of organizations—that's who I am. That is a highly focused and condensed statement of my talents, values, and guiding principles. It is a reflection, in words, that I find completely harmonious with the true substance of my inner self.

Anytime I think of the phrase "build people and build organizations," I feel energized. I feel purposeful. When I come away from an experience of helping build people or build an organization, I feel immense satisfaction and self-fulfillment. I have a strong emotional response to the phrase "build people and build organizations."

Your life-purpose statement should make you feel enthusiastic about life, motivated, and desirous of pursuing your goals. Your life-purpose statement should so embody who you are and what you hope to become that you feel compelled to fulfill your life purpose!

Beginning at the End

Your life-purpose statement in many ways begins at the end. A life-purpose statement is not about the beginning of a process, but what you foresee as the end of a process. Look as far down the road into your life as you can, and as deep into your heart as you can, and merge the two images. The word picture that you create should touch both who you are at your core and what you hope to become by the end of your life. Begin with the end in mind. If you can envision your life being fulfilled, you can do what it takes to reach that point.

When I look into my future, I can see myself building people and building organizations as long as I live. It is a life that excites me, and about which I feel a sense of genuine accomplishment and value. It is a life that is appealing as well as compelling to me.

What about you? What one statement reflects the life you will one day desire to have lived?

Ongoing Motivational Energy

Your life-purpose statement should energize you. I recently was working with a group of very intelligent young men. In fact, this particular group has been nationally recognized for its work in the computer field. One man in the group asked me, "What is the reason for a life-purpose statement? What is its real value to us?"

I responded to him this way: "Did you and your wife have any photographs taken of your wedding?"

He said, "Of course we did. We look at them fairly often."

I said, "How do you feel when you look at them?"

"Awesome," he said. "They make me feel as if I just fell in love with her all over again."

"Good," I said. "That's how a life-purpose statement should make you feel."

You should have an emotional response to your life-purpose statement. Your statement should motivate you, energize you, and inspire you.

Real Purpose or a By-Product?

When you know your life purpose, and then you pursue that purpose with all your heart, the things you want in life will come to you. They are by-products of your pursuing your life purpose.

Consider the person who says, "I want to be rich." That's not a purpose for living; that's a financial goal. A person who is motivated by the idea "I want to be rich" is going to engage in one scheme after the next until he "lucks into" something that seems to yield him a little money.

In contrast, consider the person who says, "I want to teach illiterate people how to read." Such a life purpose requires that a person take a look at his basic talents. Is the person gifted as a teacher? Does he enjoy communicating with others? Or is he perhaps good at business and organization to the degree he might work with a group of good teachers to implement his purpose in life?

A life purpose of "teaching illiterate people how to read" is going to involve skill development. Training in how to be a teacher and training specifically in how to teach reading are likely to be the basics. Specialization in teaching reading to children, to adults, or to non-English-speaking persons might be required.

This life purpose is also going to direct a person toward several avenues of work or service, such as teaching reading as a volunteer, teaching reading as a professional in a school setting, teaching reading as part of a missionary position, teaching reading to neighborhood boys and girls in an after-school club, or tutoring reading skills at school.

The satisfaction of fulfilling a life purpose is going to be great. And the motivation to continue in this area is going to be strong—each person who learns to read is likely to confirm that the goal is worthy and the results are intrinsically rewarding.

What would you enjoy doing even if you never earned a dime at doing it? Is there something that you do that causes you to say at the end of a day, "Wow, that was great; I had a fantastic day because I _____"?

When you pursue what you want to *be,* and what you want to be is truly rooted in your talents, then you automatically will have direction about what you ought to *do.* Not only that, but you'll want to do it!

A FOUNDATION AND A DIRECTION

The direction and answers you seek in life should flow from an awareness of who you are. Your inner self, not outer circumstances, should dictate how you choose to behave and what you choose to do.

Your talent combination, core values, life-purpose statement, and guiding principles are a fairly comprehensive reflection of the person you are. These values and statements form a composite word picture of your being, your inner self.

Anytime you are faced with a decision, a choice, a temptation, or the demand for an opinion, take a look at who you are.

Is the boss asking you to do something about which you feel uneasy? Why? Take a look at who you are. Is your boss's request in conflict with your values or life purpose? If so, recognize that your compliance with your boss's request is going to be increasingly painful and difficult for you. It isn't a "fit" with who you are.

Are you being asked to relocate to another city to take a promotion that means a change in jobs? Is that new job in keeping with your talent combination? Is the move going to be in concert with your values, or is it going to be a force attempting to erode your values?

Are you facing a decision about whether to marry a person you have been dating for several months? Take a look at who you are. Does this person share your same values? Is this a person who can help you fulfill your life purpose? Can you help fulfill theirs?

WALK THE TALK

Out of who you truly are, speak. What you speak, do.

People are looking for others around them who say the right things that resonate with what they know to be good values and strong moral character. Even more, they are looking for people whose lives embody their talk. They are looking for people who "walk the talk" of what they profess to believe and of what they claim to be.

Now, no person can say the right thing all the time or walk

in perfection. It's simply not possible. But we can seek to say the right thing as often as possible and walk the talk to the best of our ability.

Half of all Americans said in a recent poll that they could not follow a leader who does not walk the talk. We all desire to see people in the public eye who stand for something noble. Even more, we desire to see those people live in a noble manner. Their lives give validity to their words. So often we think that our words validate our lives—the very opposite is true. Our lives validate what we say and what we hold to be our most enduring values and our highest purpose for being.

The pursuit of personal greatness begins when you get your cart before the horse, and begin being before doing.

BLOW YOUR MIND

UNLIKE SOME OF MY PEERS, I CONSIDER MYSELF FORtunate to have experienced the late 1960s. What an interesting period to observe, to live through, and to have learned from! Hippies, flower children, and all sorts of other people were roaming our planet seeking "truth" in those years. Some turned to Eastern religions, some to free love, and a good number to drugs, including hallucination-producing compounds. The mantra of those who dropped acid (LSD) or smoked pot seemed to be, "Hey, man, you gotta blow your mind!"

Blowing one's mind was perceived to be the key to finding a new reality, a new depth of seeing and understanding the world. It was considered the way to see beyond the Establishment to a new order supposedly marked by harmony, peace, love, and understanding.

In the end, the Eastern religions, sex, and drugs of the 1960s didn't create a new order that was any better than any other order of the past, but the phrase "blow your mind" continues to be heard in our culture. In today's terminology, if something "blows your mind," it tends to startle you, shock you, confound you, or even exhilarate you—generally to the point of causing you to see things in a new light. There's great power in blowing a mind wide open to a new reality.

Among the many gifts God has given to each of us, the mind certainly has to rank near the top. The mind is so powerful that one thought can change a life. Thoughts are the essence of our dreams, our creativity, our motivation. When we put plans to our thoughts, and then take action on them, great things happen in our lives!

We must realize that the mind also has a tendency to "lock in" to certain ways of thinking, for better or worse. It doesn't take long for a person to begin to believe that the way he thinks is the way life really *is*—period. What a person thinks becomes his understanding of reality, and what the person understands to be real *is* real—at least to that individual. Once the mind has locked into a set of beliefs and values, a person rarely challenges the way he thinks.

Earlier I shared with you the story of James, who was told he was not CEO material. James was gripped by that statement made to him by the executives of his parent company. It haunted him. Deep down in his soul he began to believe it was true. Then came the day we sat down on the park bench, and our conversation began a process that blew James's mind. He began to reject his old thinking patterns. He blew the old thoughts out of his mind and started over with right thinking patterns. The more he blew away the old thoughts that were holding him back, the more liberated he felt and the more he began to move into his potential.

If I shared with you all the examples of people I know, or those I have read about in history, who have chosen to reengineer how they think, this book would be so thick you couldn't even hold it. Consider a Founding Father such as Thomas Jefferson, an explorer such as Columbus, a scientist such as Albert Einstein, a civil rights leader such as Martin Luther King Jr.—the list could go on and on. Their respective marks on history began with an idea.

If you have locked into the idea that you cannot become great, then today is the day you need to blow your mind. That's right—blow out the old way of thinking, and start over.

Not long ago I encountered a group of young executives who had a mind-blowing experience. These young executives work for a firm run by a father and son. The business has prospered in recent years, and several new, young, energetic partners have joined the firm.

These partners had become divided over the behavior of the father. Several of them said to me privately, "I don't understand why he doesn't play by the same rules the rest of us have to follow. He comes in when he wants, leaves when he wants, and conducts business in a manner quite different from the rest of us."

One day I got all the partners together in a room, and I asked them as a group, "Is Marvin a hard worker?"

"The hardest," they all said in agreement.

"Is Marv a big producer?"

They agreed: "He bills more than anyone in the firm."

"Does Marv have many valuable business contracts?"

Again they agreed: "Absolutely. He has more than you can imagine."

"OK," I said, "I have just one more question."

"What's that?" they asked as they eagerly moved forward in their seats.

"Who founded this company?"

"Marv," they said, somewhat puzzled at where I might be going.

"That's exactly right," I said. "Marvin is the founder. You guys will never have another founder. By definition, there is only one founder. You all think he should behave like you do when that is impossible. He is behaving like the *founder* that he is."

I wish you could have seen the looks on their faces. These strong, smart, educated, highly motivated, extremely successful men and women looked at me with astonishment and revelation on their faces. They finally saw what they had needed to see! Their minds had been blown open to the point where they understood that being a founder is a once-in-a-lifetime, unique role. A founder has responsibilities, privileges, obligations, and rights that no follower ever has.

That one idea blew their minds. That one idea immediately and dramatically changed their outlook and the way they thought about themselves, their company, and their leader. That one thought completely dissolved the disharmony that had reached almost a crisis level. Since then, these executives have moved in harmony, and their growth has been strong.

Marv still does his thing—in his way, in his timing, and with his personality at full strength—but their response to him is no longer one of conflict and resentment. They respond now with appreciation and support.

What Ideas Need to Be Blown Away?

Your mind has already been trained to some extent and in a certain direction. No person reading this book has an untrained mind. Your mind has been trained to read, to speak, to think, to reason, to make decisions, and to solve problems. You do so according to patterns that you have learned through repeated experiences. The habits of your thinking have already been established.

Ten Concepts for Reengineering Your Thinking (Blowing Your Mind)

Let me share with you ten basic concepts that are related to the way you think about yourself and the achievement of personal greatness.

1. Think Differently and Uniquely

Those who achieve personal greatness think differently and uniquely. They value their distinct selves—they do not see themselves as followers of predetermined cultural norms.

How do you think? The way everybody else does? According to world systems? According to the culture portrayed on television or in movies?

Refuse to accept the current status of your thought life. Reevaluate how you think and why you think the way you do.

Choose to think

- *differently.* Choose to think out of your values, not out of cultural norms. Choose to think at the highest end of values, not at the level of the least common denominator.

- *uniquely.* Embrace your originality and creativity.

Every person is unique—one of a kind, but we all operate under unchanging natural laws. Gravity is gravity is gravity. God's natural laws are universal, from one generation to the next and from one culture to the next. His laws are absolute.

But the *application* of His principles—the manifestation of His grace, purpose, and plan—is distinctively unique to each person. God never does the same thing twice in precisely the same way. Through nature, He makes billions upon billions of snowflakes every winter, and the general characteristics of these snowflakes are alike in the basics of design, function, and origin. Yet every snowflake is unique—a one-of-a-kind design that has never been seen before and will never be seen again.

People are alike in many ways—we all have hearts and brains and fears and hopes. Yet every person is unique, a one-of-a-kind creation with a completely original DNA pattern. No two fingerprints or handprints are alike, no two footprints are alike, no two voiceprints are alike, no two patterns in the iris of the eye are alike, and no two sets of circumstances or composite sets of life experiences are exactly alike. Each person lives in a unique context of time and space from the moment of birth.

And so, too, our thinking is unique. Each person has a unique, one-of-a-kind set of dreams, goals, desires, propensities, and wishes. You may have some dreams in common with others, but your dream for your life will always have unique components to it and your overall set of dreams, goals, and desires will be unique. Dreams and goals will be in varying combinations, with emphases in distinct areas. Your imagination will be directed into unique ideas.

We've all heard the comment: "There's nothing new under the sun." That's true in a general way. It is equally true that everything is new under the sun. Millions upon millions of never-before-uttered sentences are going to be spoken today, in contexts that have never been experienced before, by people who know the same basic vocabulary words but who string them together in original ways. Poets are going to spin old, familiar words into new combinations. Artists are going to use the ages-old spectrum of color and light to create works that have never been seen before. Musicians are going to use a very limited number of notes on the musical scale to create new tunes.

Open your mind to your unique thoughts—thoughts that are different from those of the world at large, thoughts that are different from those of the person in the cubicle next to you, thoughts that may seem completely "out of the box" even to you!

Dare to think thoughts and dream dreams that are not mundane and ordinary.

2. Embrace the Renewing of Your Thoughts

Those who achieve personal greatness constantly pursue a renewal of their minds.

Your mental transformation requires your participation. Renewal is not something that happens instantly or apart from your will. Renewal is a process that follows a certain pattern. It requires reflection upon the very best of ideas. It requires application—it requires that you act on the best of what you know. Much of what you learn comes through doing.

If I tell you something, you have only a 50 percent chance of remembering it. If I tell you something as I illustrate what I say, you have an 80 percent likelihood of remembering it. But if you act on something I tell you and show you—if you do something, and especially if you do it at your own initiation—you are nearly 100 percent likely to remember it.

Have you ever been in the grip of something sinister, such as a drug addiction, alcoholism, or deep debt? If you have, you know that it's difficult to think at length about something other than the problem. The problem is always present, frequently coming to mind through recurring urges or fears.

Numerous other obsessions and desires are less intense, but nonetheless ingrained in our thought processes. Greed for things we want to own, lust for a person who is not rightfully ours, an insatiable desire for power or fame, a compelling drive toward manipulation or conquest in order to elevate our self-importance—all of these thoughts tend to grab hold of the mind and refuse to let go. They become our reasons for being—more money, more promotions, more visibility, more possessions, more authority, more awards.

I certainly believe we are to be blessed materially. I also clearly recognize that organizations are based upon line authority and that organizational charts have value in getting a task accomplished. I am in favor of self-improvement and personal growth. But when any self-gratifying or self-glorifying desire begins to take over a person's thought process, that person is in need of renewal.

As stated earlier, the renewal process involves two basic steps: reflection upon being the right things, and active engagement in doing the right things.

The Bible gives directives about the thought life:

> Whatever things are true, whatever things are noble, whatever things are just, whatever things are pure, whatever things are lovely, whatever things are of good report, if there is any virtue and if there is anything praiseworthy—meditate on these things. (Phil. 4:8)

It's up to you to choose what you will think about. It's up to you to choose the subjects on which you will allow your mind to dwell. It's up to you to choose the topics about which you will study, discuss, or daydream. Take charge of your thought processes. Actively and intentionally choose only the very best input to your mind.

Don't just meditate on the right things, however; *do* the right things. Seek to manifest your best ideas in the day-to-day practicalities of life.

Is it a good thing to be courageous? Absolutely. I don't know anyone who would disagree with the value of that character trait. How do you become more courageous? First, seek out, read, and meditate on stories of courage in other people. Steep yourself in words that inspire courage in your heart. Focus on the positive—consider what it takes to live a noble, brave life of self-sacrifice. And then every day seek to exercise your courage. Talk to the person to whom you've been afraid to talk. Ask a question you've been afraid to ask. Help a person who needs your help, even if you are uncertain of the person's response. Speak a word of encouragement to the person you have passed in silence for months, perhaps years.

Small acts of courage position a person to demonstrate greater acts of courage. Don't wait for a heroic opportunity to arrive. Rather, go out and create heroic moments.

What is the end result of doing deeds that require courage, and of reflecting intentionally and regularly on stories of courage? Greater courage! The renewed mind moves away from fear and toward belief and courageous action.

Identify the areas in your thought life that need renewal. Do you have the right opinion of God? Do you have the right opinion of yourself? Do you have the right opinion of other people? Do you have the right attitude toward those who have hurt you, rejected you, or criticized you? Do you know how to respond to crises and troubles? What about your thinking needs to be adjusted so that you will think and respond to life in the ways you should.

Make a sober judgment about your thinking. Choose to think differently. Choose to be renewed. And then . . .

3. Think About the Link Between Your Life Purpose and Your Talents

Those who achieve personal greatness know themselves, and they live true to their purpose and gifts.

Why do you exist? I realize this is a question that philosophers have been asking since time began. It is a question that many of us grapple with from time to time, very often without coming to a satisfactory conclusion.

I believe the answer to this question lies in taking a look at your talents, abilities, and deepest desires.

What is the purpose of a hammer? To hammer nails.

What is the purpose of a saw? To cut wood.

What is the purpose of a pitcher? To pour liquid.

What is the purpose of an oven? To cook food.

See yourself as a tool—an instrument to unlock the potential within the lives of others. What talents has God given you? What are you naturally gifted to do with minimal effort and maximum joy? What gifts do you most enjoy developing or practicing? What is easy for you to learn?

Identify your gifts, and you'll know what to do. Identify your abilities and your desires, and you'll know your life purpose. Identify your capacities and capabilities, and you'll know why your Creator put you on this planet at precisely this time in history.

A person who is good at writing should be a writer.

A person who is gifted in music should be a musician.

A person who is gifted at organizing should be a manager.

Apart from your talents, you have been given a measure of intelligence.

Other indexes of individual traits, such as personality types, may be useful in identifying precisely who you have been created to be. Add to those indexes a thorough, introspective appraisal of what you desire to see accomplished, changed in, or eliminated from this world. Ask yourself such questions as:

- *What would I most like to see changed in my immediate world?*

- *What is the most pressing need that I see?*

- *Where is there a weakness or breakdown that needs to be strengthened or mended?*

- *What energizes me the most? What gives me the greatest emotional high with regard to helping other people?*

Think about who God has created you to be. Think about what motivates you, encourages you, dismays you, and energizes you. Think about how your gifts, intelligence, and personality might be focused on a purpose greater than your own sustenance or maintenance. Think about *why* God has placed you on this earth at this precise time in the exact environment in which you find yourself.

When taken as a whole, your unique set of traits and desires should point you in the direction of what you are to do with your life. Your individual traits and desires are the undergirding elements of your life-purpose statement.

4. Think About Your Capacity for Greatness

Those who achieve personal greatness see themselves as capable of accomplishing big goals.

Many people sell themselves short in this area. Virtually all people realize that they have a capacity for receiving and giving, growing and developing, attaining and achieving; they simply don't grasp how much capacity they have.

The truth is we have all been born with the capacity for greatness—it is a gift to each of us from God. In my opinion, the vast majority of people on this earth haven't begun to think about all that has been prepared for them to experience, exert authority over, possess, use, accomplish, establish, create, or perform in a lifetime. Stop to think about your capacity, your ability, your capability, and your deep longing to embrace more of life.

Recognize, too, that your capacity and ability are God-given. I am continually amazed at the people who tell me with confidence that they have a relationship with almighty God—infinite in power, strength, wisdom, understanding, and love—and then tell me with equal chagrin that they don't believe they can raise their level of performance. They fail to see that God's omnipotent, omniscient power residing in them gives them an extra edge when it comes to capacity and ability.

Our human potential is no longer merely human ability once we have energized it through our faith. Our ability at that point becomes not a matter of what we can do, but what God can enable us to do. There's a huge difference. Man may have limited ability, but with God, the ceiling on ability is removed. With God, *all* things become possible.

The more you believe in your talent and realize that it is greater than you think it is, the more you will feel an inner drive to pursue your potential to become great.

5. Think of Risk in Terms of Success

Those who achieve personal greatness take risks with a full expectation of success.

We tend to avoid unknown territory or risks because we are afraid we will not succeed. We don't take risks because we ask ourselves, *What are the chances I'll fail?*

Turn that around. Change your thinking. Ask yourself,

What are the chances I'll succeed if I work long enough and hard enough at this? In all probability, the chances are high!

The actual percentage of people who totally fail when they try something is very small. The fact is, if a mentally and emotionally healthy person is willing to take a risk or enter an unknown territory, that person is usually cautious enough to weigh various factors related to the risk and to make preparations in advance of taking the risk. The result is nearly always some measure of success. Accidents in timing and circumstances are always possible, but even in the vast majority of those instances, failure can usually produce a measure of learning so that future success is more likely.

I met a man who had dreamed his entire life of being involved in the theater. He wanted to be an actor, and his dream was to work in theatrical productions that would have a powerful spiritual impact on people's lives. He "stuffed" that dream for nearly a decade because he couldn't see how he could make a living doing what he longed to do. Instead, he became a successful salesman.

The desire to be onstage didn't leave him, however, and after about ten years of being out of the theater world, he became involved in community theater productions. He got some bit parts, then a leading role, and then a string of leading roles. He grew in his acting ability.

And then, more than twenty-five years after he left the college theatrical world, he was given an opportunity to become involved full-time in a theatrical production that was directly aimed at his life's dream.

Was it a risk for this man to leave his successful sales career and embark on a full-time acting career? Yes. Was he scared of failure? He wasn't fearful of failing as an actor nearly as much as he was afraid of failing financially, but yes, he was fearful. Did he take the risk anyway? Yes.

For the past seven years he has worked full-time as an actor. He has had leading roles in three major shows in one of the major resort centers of America. He has influenced countless thousands of people to think more deeply about their relationships with God. And he feels greater fulfillment in his life with each passing month. His purpose for living has finally come to the point of fruition, and he is bearing a bumper harvest of good fruit.

The biggest obstacle to your pursuit of your potential and purpose in life is likely to be the fear of taking a risk. Think about that fear. Confront it. Refuse to embrace it. Bolster yourself with courage. And change your thinking—move from "risk of failure" to "risk of success" thinking!

6. See the Pathway Between Your Mind and Your Heart

Those who achieve personal greatness are not afraid to embrace or express their emotions.

Whether they know it or not, most people live in their minds. Our external life is, to a very great extent, determined by how well we think. Our thinking enables us to manipulate the world—for good or for bad. Our thinking gives rise to our words, which enable us to influence others. Very few people have learned to live truly from their hearts.

The greater perspective is this: a person doesn't respond to life from either the mind or the heart. A person responds from both. Most of us hold to the opinion that we think with our minds and feel with our hearts. If you ask a person to isolate the processes, however, he eventually must come to the conclusion: we respond to life simultaneously with our thoughts and feelings from the inside out.

In the wake of the September 11 attack on the Twin Towers of the World Trade Center in New York City, I asked a number of people their first reaction to seeing those buildings in flames, especially their reaction at seeing an airplane fly directly into the second of the towers that were hit that morning. Almost every person said, in effect, "For a split second, I couldn't believe what I was seeing. Then I felt a sick horror in the pit of my stomach, and I thought, *Oh, my God. This was intentional.*" Feelings and thoughts, and even an awareness of a need for prayer and help from the Almighty, were instinctive and immediate. Feelings and thoughts were not separated.

Most of the character traits that we all value—love, compassion, fairness, gratitude, bravery, self-giving—are traits that are a wonderful mixture of what we believe and what we feel. What we do is rarely motivated solely by a great idea. Neither is our motivation rooted solely in a strong feeling. The two are intended to go hand in hand—with our feelings driving our energy as our ideas focus that energy.

As you think about who you are and what you are uniquely equipped and called to do in your life, don't rule out the role of your heart. The Bible tells us this about human nature: "As he thinks in his heart, so is he" (Prov. 23:7). As you allow your deepest feelings and opinions to be manifested in outward actions, you reach your personal destiny.

7. *Think of Life As a Process.*

Those who achieve personal greatness regard life as a process of personal character development that does not end.

Through the years, the vast majority of people I've met have come to my seminars and training sessions with a pre-conceived idea that life is a series of events. Work tends to be regarded as a series of projects to be identified, performed, and shelved away. Work is deadline and task driven. The line worker who is involved in the mass production of widgets is just as likely to think this way as the software engineer who is creating a new technology.

But far greater than any project or series of projects is the *process* of life. Life is about who we become. Life is about the character we develop and the influence we exert far more than it is about the projects we complete or the awards we hang on our walls.

A couple of years ago, I went through a sad time during which two people who were very close to me died. I couldn't help but notice during that period that everything around me kept moving—cars kept driving by, work kept getting done, games kept being played. The world barely noticed my absence from the routine. Nobody commented on my empty parking space, my empty office, or my empty seat among the season ticket holders.

Our nation took a serious hit on September 11, 2001, with the destruction of the World Trade Center, the damage to the Pentagon, and the crashing of four hijacked airplanes. No doubt about it—we were reeling as a nation. For several days, things stopped. Commercial air traffic was grounded. The financial markets were closed. Games and broadcast events and conventions were canceled. Theme parks and shopping malls were emptied. Normal work processes came to an abrupt halt—but only temporarily.

One week after that tragedy of tragedies in our nation's history, flights were taking off and landing, stocks were being traded, games were being played, purchases were being rung up, and roller coasters were rumbling. The processes of life resumed. Weddings and funerals were held.

There are events that have caused some people to give up and say, "I'm going to quit trying"; "I don't believe in people anymore"; "I'm not going to trust anymore." On the positive side, there are some events that cause people to make declarations and vow, "I'm going to give up that bad habit," or "I'm going to risk loving again." But events and decisions such as these also give way to process. It's one thing to decide to give up a bad habit, and quite another thing to give up that habit day after day after day after day. It's one thing to say, "I give up"—and another to then be confronted by a sun that comes up tomorrow and tomorrow and tomorrow and tomorrow.

Shortly after my mother's death, Don George, a pastor and dear friend of mine, gave me a copy of a book that described a vision of heaven that was experienced by a woman in the 1920s. One of the concepts in the book was this: wherever you are in your learning process on the earth, that is where you pick up learning in heaven. Learning goes on. Believing goes on. Growing continues.

We never stop *becoming*. It is at the heart of life's processes. There's always more to explore and discover, more to know and understand, more to experience, more to develop and change and improve.

Embrace the process! It is in these ongoing processes of life—now, and very likely, for all eternity—that we build our integrity and character. It is in the processes of life that we establish and exercise our faith. It is in the processes of life that we grow and mature in the inner man. It is in the processes of life that we develop and manifest our reputation. It is in the processes of life that we love and are loved.

It is in the processes of life that we become great.

Reflect thoughtfully on the overall flow of your life and the traits that mark how you live, what you stand for, and the choices you make that continue to influence those around you.

8. Move Toward a Principle-Centered Life

Those who achieve personal greatness understand that there is a difference in the style of a person's personality and the core values related to a life of principle. Let me explain.

I once consulted for a fairly well-known personality in the United States. He was a rather controversial person—many people loved him; others were very suspicious of his motives.

At times when a person learned that I was working with his organization, I would hear the question, "Is he genuine?"

I usually asked, "What do you mean by that?"

I'd hear comments such as: "Look at how he dresses. Look at the car he drives. I've heard he lives in a fancy house."

My response was this: "Those sound like style issues to me. What I know with certainty is that he is a truthful man, he is a good husband and father, and he is faithful to his friends. Don't look at the packaging of his personality. Look at the principles of his character."

I believe that is the criterion by which we should evaluate all people and the situations in which we find ourselves. Are we caught up in the packaging of personality? Are we consumed with how we look, what we drive, where we live, and the personal objects we possess? Or are we intent on deter-mining the principles of character at work? Is the person hon-est? Does he work hard? Is he trustworthy? Is he motivated to do good to others? Does he tell the truth? Is he manipulative and power hungry? Is he biased or fair-minded?

Style comes and goes. Character lasts. The principles by which we live exert influence on others long after we are gone.

I talked to a friend who was the executor of an estate. She told me that all of her friend's possessions were disseminated within a matter of a few weeks. More than thirty families had readily absorbed her belongings, many of which were beautiful artifacts from around the world. And then she said, "But we still recall things she did, and we imagine her response to various world events as well as to various events in our personal lives. We can almost hear her laugh, her admonitions, her truth-filled quips. We can see her expressions in the mind's eye. Who she *was* will never be scattered. It is very focused in our memories."

Your principles will live on in your children and grand-children as well as in your friends, colleagues, clients, parish-ioners, vendors, patrons, and even those who observe your life from afar.

A strong personality is not the same as a strong character. The same holds true for a strong will. Nothing can equal the impact of a strong character.

Reflect today on the principles that are at the core of your life. Reflect on the definition that you desire for your charac-ter. Reflect on how you want others to think of you and remember you after you are gone.

9. Live for a Purpose Larger Than Yourself

Those who achieve personal greatness hook their thinking and their lives into a cause or purpose that is bigger than the meeting of their basic needs.

God's purpose for your life extends beyond you. His purpose begins in you, but it never ends with you.

I can't tell you what that purpose may be. There are a million or more good purposes or causes or missions. You will need to define what commands your attention, challenges your faith, compels your interest, and convicts you to act.

The best cause for you to choose is one that is in sync with your unique set of desires, goals, talents, intelligence, and interests. It is likely to be a purpose that flows from and is related to your past experiences, your present level of skills, and your personal environment.

At the same time, I caution you to weigh carefully the opportunities that others will give you to volunteer. People will come to you offering noble purposes or causes. Don't let the persuasive personality of another person dictate to you the area in which you should give your time, talents, or resources. Make your choice based upon your desires, personal purpose in life, and conviction of heart. Only the causes that you pursue because you have a heart-felt drive to see them succeed will continue to captivate your attention and interest over time.

Think about what you consider to be the greatest purpose worthy of your time, talents, and material resources.

10. Choose to Become Generous in Every Area of Your Life

Those who achieve personal greatness never think they lose or are less as a result of their giving.

Those who are selfish, self-focused, or arrogant do not succeed in the long run. They may be able to exert power to succeed in short-term situations, but their influence over time is not positive. The greatest reputations are awarded to those who serve others.

Countless people in this world are in pursuit of a career goal, a marker of financial success, a position or title or office. Their approach is, "I don't care what it takes or who I need to step on to get there." They don't realize that the moment they reach that goal, win that election, or assume that lofty position, everything related to their success will be directly related to who they have stepped on and how they have pursued their rise to the top. What they have sown is ultimately what they will reap.

Choose to be a giver. A giver of sincere compliments and praise for good achievement. A giver of rewards and awards and recognition. A giver of your time and presence to persons in need. A giver of your resources to worthy causes. A giver of encouragement.

When you are motivated by helping others become successful—seeing their needs met, their goals reached, and their dreams fulfilled—you will be successful as a by-product of your service. God's basic law of reciprocity is encapsulated in these passages of Scripture:

There is one who scatters, yet increases more. (Prov. 11:24)

Give, and it will be given to you: good measure, pressed down, shaken together, and running over . . . For with the same measure that you use, it will be measured back to you. (Luke 6:38)

Whatever a man sows, that he will also reap . . . And let us not grow weary while doing good, for in due season we shall reap if we do not lose heart. Therefore, as we have opportunity, let us do good to all, especially to those who are of the household of faith. (Gal. 6:7–10)

To live in a miserly, self-centered way results in an extremely hollow, unfulfilled life.

Think today about ways in which you can give more of yourself to help someone else succeed.

NOTHING HAPPENS UNTIL YOU BELIEVE

You have the ability to renew your thinking processes.

You have the ability to change the way you have been thinking.

You have the ability to connect the pathway between your mind and your heart so that the decisions you make with your mind are consonant with the values you hold in your heart.

Furthermore, you have the *responsibility* for engaging in the renewal of your mind. You must choose renewal. You must engage in the activities that bring about renewal.

Most of all, you must believe that it is possible for a person to change the way he thinks.

The struggle to take charge of every thought may be difficult—it may even feel like a war on the inside—but the struggle is vital and the end result is worthy of the fight!

You are a victim of your environment only if you continue to believe you are.

You are a victim of circumstances only if you continue to think you are.

You are a victim of old hurts and wounds only if you continue to claim in your mind and heart that you are a victim.

Our minds are ours to conquer.

Virtually every person who becomes a success in any area of life first believes he can be a success.

Virtually every person who becomes financially independent and lives free of debt first believes he can become financially independent.

Virtually every person who becomes a great leader first believes he can influence others in a positive way.

WALK TOWARD THE BARKING DOG

WHEN I WAS A BOY, MY WALK TO SCHOOL LED ME PAST a house with a ferocious dog. At least that's the way the dog appeared to me. I mustered my courage every morning to withstand the onslaught of barking and charging that I knew was sure to come if the dog spotted me. I prepared myself to run as fast as I could down the street until the dog gave up and returned home. And I hoped each morning that this day I might sneak past him without incident.

This pattern went on for months.

Then one morning, without any explanation that I can rationally deduce, I decided that I had had enough of this barking dog. The dog hadn't changed. It still came charging at me with nostrils flared, fangs bared, and barks blaring, but *I* had changed. Rather than run in fear, I calmly turned and charged toward the dog with stick in hand and shouts of my own.

To my surprise, and also to my immense relief, the dog stopped abruptly in its tracks, and then turned and hightailed it back to the recesses of its yard. It never bothered me again.

Life is filled with barking dogs. Big challenges and little

ones. Major problems and minor ones. Some are lifethreatening, and some are just threatening to one's peace of mind, material security, or emotional well-being.

IT'S NOT THE SIZE OF THE DOG THAT COUNTS

It's not the size of the dog that counts. Small dogs can nip at the heels and cause us to run just as fast as when big dogs snarl in our direction and cause us to panic.

The fact is, we all face barking, snarling, nipping, charging dogs at some point—big and small, some more fierce than others. What counts is our response.

What barking dog are you facing today?

A coworker who routinely answers your phone but fails to take and leave accurate messages?

A diagnosis of cancer?

A neighbor who consistently allows trash to blow into your yard?

A termination notice from a major client?

A child who is rebellious, regardless of the topic at hand or the authority figure in charge?

A runaway spouse?

A teacher who ignores your preschooler day in and day out?

A stack of unpaid bills and a lousy credit rating?

I don't know the barking dog in your life. You may be surrounded by barking dogs!

What I do know is this: the dog will continue to bark until you do something about it. In most cases, the solution is not to run from it in fear, hoping to outdistance it or wish it away, but to charge the barking dog. Embrace the challenge. Confront the problem head-on and with all of your energy.

Taking on Adversity

Perhaps the foremost opportunity to display a positive influence and genuine personal greatness presents itself when we face adversity. When things are going our way and we are living on the sunny side of the street, we tend to spend very little time asking ourselves, *Am I doing the right thing? Am I doing the best I can do to help others? Am I truly displaying the values I hold to be true?* When tragedy strikes, however, we nearly always come face-to-face with these questions as well as the ultimate question related to our influence, *Why is this happening? Is it the result of something I didn't do that I should have done?*

Adversity is the prime time in our lives to demonstrate moral character and right values.

The fact is, adversity comes to all of us in varying doses at varying times of our lives. We do our best to shield ourselves from adversity. We buckle our seat belts and buy cars with airbags. We build retirement funds so we won't face an impoverished old age, and we build savings funds so we won't suffer overwhelming loss if tragedy strikes. We buy insurance policies as a hedge against adversity. But in the end, all of us suffer some adversity in life. Nobody can "life-proof" himself and still remain alive!

If adversity is inevitable, then we must have a means of accommodating it. We must have a way of holding it in our minds and hearts. We can see it as an opportunity to grow and develop as a person, or we can see it as something that destroys us. We can see it as something that can bring us bene-fit in the long run, or we can see it as something that over-whelms us. In sum, there are principles involved in the way we handle adversity.

Embrace Adversity As a Forging Tool

A leader embraces adversity as a forging tool in life. Most people do their utmost to avoid adversity. Some deny any benefit associated with adversity. A leader, in contrast, evalu-ates the situation, reconnects with his greater purpose in life, seeks to create options for handling the adversity, and then takes action to create his future beyond the adversity.

I don't like the way adversity makes me feel when it comes into my life, but I have learned that if I see adversity as an opportunity for refinement and growth, it takes on a whole new character. It is no longer something to be shunned, but something to be overcome, endured, and perhaps embraced.

A close friend of mine learned that his wife had breast cancer. She had gone to her physician after finding a lump in her breast. A nurse had called after the exam to ask if the doctor had called yet. He hadn't. She said, "Well, no call is probably a good sign. It was probably just a lump or cyst that will dissolve on its own." My friend and his wife had rejoiced at that call, only to have their joy collapse ninety minutes later when the physician called and said, "You have cancer, and you need to come to the clinic right away."

They asked many *why* questions in the days that followed: "Why did this happen?" "Why us?" "Why now?" Then my friend said, "We realized that we were asking far more *why* questions than *how* questions. As a child, I rarely asked *why*. I asked *how*. How can I learn to ride this bicycle? How can I solve this math problem? How can I fix this broken radio?

"I thought, *I need to be more childlike in this.* Breast cancer has happened to my wife and to us as a couple. How do we get through this? How do we deal with the cancer as a physical growth that doesn't belong in her body? How can we deal emotionally with the fact that my wife has cancer? How can we find and then get in touch with the best people to help us on both the physical-medical and the emotional-spiritual fronts? When we turned our focus from *why* to *how,* we began to move forward in a positive way."

It is nearly always more beneficial to ask *what, how, where, who,* and *when* questions than to ask *why* questions when adversity strikes. The fact is, we often do not have answers to *why* questions—and might never have answers to them this side of eternity. We are endowed, however, with the ability for answering *who, what, when, how,* and *where* questions.

Adversity is also a prime time to reach out to others—to ask for help, to give help, to shoulder burdens alongside others. In the instance I just described, my friend and his wife made a pact: "Some days you are going to be discouraged, and I promise to be there to pick you up. Occasionally I might be discouraged, and you are going to need to be there to help me up. If we both get down, we are going to help each other." They made an agreement to do their very best to encourage each other.

Along the way, they entered a partnership of treatment. They reached agreement about the course of medical care the wife was to receive, including the foods she would eat and the exercises she would do. The husband agreed to eat the same foods and do the same exercises. During the course of her radiation treatments, he cooked most of the family meals. They walked together. They talked about positive things as they ate and exercised together.

Many times we find that we can believe for recovery from a major blow, but the pathway to recovery is not clear to us. Of one thing I am certain: it is rarely the right thing to wander off on one's own for extended periods of time. Prolonged isolation leads only to alienation, which is never the right thing in a relationship that is valued and rooted in love.

Part of this couple's agreement was an agreement to be patient with each other, and to be patient with the healing process. They never gave up in their faith. They pursued health with deep faith. But they knew the greater threat to them was not a lack of faith but a lack of patience. So they agreed to do their utmost to promote patience in each other.

This did not keep them from pursuing health with energy and focus—it simply meant that they gave the healing process time. They didn't force the cure, they didn't require instant results, and they didn't expect overnight success. They were willing to walk out the long path rather than take shortcuts. They knew that to set up false expectations and artificial deadlines was only to set themselves up for disappointment, which produces stress. And stress is well documented as being counterproductive to healing.

Patience is always the right thing to have in your relationships with other people—including those with whom you work. No company is an overnight success. It's a little like the entertainer who once said, "They call me an overnight success. Well, that 'overnight' occurred after twenty years of singing my heart out in every venue open to me." Overcoming adversity often requires enduring patience.

John Templeton of the Templeton Funds is one of the greatest financial advisers and fund managers in history. He was born and raised in Tennessee and, as a young boy, had virtually nothing of material advantage. In his life, however, he accumulated billions.

What was Templeton's strategy? The first thing he looked for was adversity. He found a company that was experiencing a difficulty and that had leaders motivated to overcome the difficulty. Both adversity and motivation to overcome adversity are intangibles. They have nothing to do directly with profit-and-loss statements, stock prices, or dividend payments. Templeton knew, however, that adversity and a high motivational level for overcoming adversity are a great combination.

Next, Templeton believed in patience. He knew that turning adversity into success took time.

Adversity, motivation to overcome adversity, and patience to endure until adversity is overcome—that's a powerful one-two-three combination.

See Adversity As an Opportunity for Personal Growth

I know a number of people whose lives are marked by great adversity.

I know parents who have trained their children in good moral values only to see their children fall under the negative influence of others as adults and become major drug dealers or drug users.

I know people who have had their lives threatened with physical violence because of a moral stance they have taken, or because of the success they have achieved.

I know people who have been robbed at gunpoint or have had their possessions stolen.

I know people who have lost their businesses or who have been cheated or defrauded by their clients or vendors.

I know people who have been abandoned by a spouse, disowned by a parent, or rejected by a child—very often without provocation on their parts.

I know people who have had major diseases, some of which have been labeled "terminal."

Some of these people have been derailed or destroyed internally by adversity.

Other people have chosen to see adversity as an opportunity for personal growth. They have actively and zealously pursued recovery, wholeness, healing, or reconciliation. They have ardently gone in search of ways to emerge from the adversity stronger and better. The result is that adversity has turned weak character traits into strong virtues. The fires of adversity have purified them.

OVERCOMING A DISCOURAGING SLUMP OR PLATEAU

One day while I was talking to my good friend Andy Murray, we began to reflect on the fact that our lives had been extremely busy in recent years as we had started new business ventures. Andy had founded a company named Brandworks, and he had taken it from zero to several million dollars in annual gross income in just a few years. He then merged his company with another firm and took a different role—moving from creator to builder and sustainer.

He said to me that day, "Things have taken a different turn, Tim. All of the start-up energy seems to have hit the mark. The pace is now slower. Things aren't popping the way they did even a few months ago—I've probably gone from a hundred miles per hour to a more sane seventy miles per hour, but I feel at times as if I'm at a dead stop. That's a new feeling for me."

"So how are you responding to this new, slower pace?" I asked.

"At first," he said, "I was very anxious about it. I almost didn't know what to do with all of the excess energy I had. But then in my devotional time, I came to Psalm 23. I've known that psalm all my life. This time, however, I began to reflect on it a little more deeply, taking it verse by verse. I came to the verse 'He makes me to lie down in green pastures; He leads me beside the still waters' [Ps. 23:2]."

"What did that verse mean to you?" I asked.

"I began to question, *Why would God make me lie down? Why would He lead me to still waters?* It was obvious to me that I felt as if I was in a 'lying down' mode. I could only assume that the Lord wanted me to be at rest—to be in a position of coming up with new ideas, rejuvenating myself physically, mentally, creatively, and emotionally from the hectic pace of the last few years."

"What about the still waters?"

"That was a puzzler. But then one morning I asked myself, *What happens to a sheep when he leans over to drink from a stream that is very still?* I reflected on that awhile, and the thought came, *That sheep sees his own reflection! He sees it against the backdrop of God's great big sky, and he sees more clearly who he is.* Perhaps one of the major reasons for this slower time in my career is to enable me to truly see myself for who I am and what I am to be doing."

What a tremendous insight! And what a tremendous blessing it is to the person whom God makes to lie down in green pastures and whom He leads to still waters.

I had a similar time in my life. I had worked for and with a man to build a major enterprise that had been very successful and was growing rapidly and powerfully. And then it seemed as if the man who was my partner hit a self-destruct button. In the course of a couple of months, the organization we had built together fizzled. It was as if the air had been let out of a large balloon—no major explosion, just a crazy, out-of-control, all-over-the-sky diminishing of resources, purpose, and influence.

I was made to lie down for a while. For several months, I questioned whether God was angry with me. Indeed, I had to admit to myself that I could have done a few things differently, but in the end, I had not been the one to sabotage the organization by my actions or words. I felt fully forgiven by God for whatever wrong I might have committed. I knew in my mind that God loved me. But in my heart, I still felt frustrated, estranged from my life's purpose, disappointed, and a little adrift.

During that time, I did the only thing I knew to do. Apart from picking up and making sense of the financial pieces and working to pay routine bills, I spent time reflecting on what I really wanted to do with my life. I spent time reflecting on who I am—the talents, personality, skills, dreams, and motivations of my life. I came face-to-face with an amazing fact: God does not have just one job for a person to do. He has a *life* for a person to live. There's a huge difference in the two statements, so let me repeat them for you:

> God does not have just one job for a person to do.
> He has a *life* for a person to live.

Personalize these statements for yourself: "God does not have just one job for me to do. He has a *life* for me to live."

Through the years, I have met countless people who are extremely wrapped up in their jobs. They are not just company men—in some cases, they are the founders or longtime CEOs of their own companies. They have spent the bulk of their working lives building an organization, a ministry, a team, or an enterprise of some type. Their work is the most fulfilling and most purposeful aspect of their lives. They can't imagine any job more rewarding or more satisfying—or in the case of ministry or nonprofit work, a job more eternally rewarding or fulfilling.

When the company folds, is bought out, or merges, or when they retire from full-time work, or perhaps when they are dismissed or replaced in a downsizing or reorganization move, each faces a genuine identity crisis. They don't truly know who they are. They feel a great loss of purpose and almost a total loss of ambition. They no longer have goals, and as part of the gearing-down process, they have no motivation, no real reason for getting up in the mornings. Anxiety, frustration, and sometimes even depression seem to come in the wake of the loss of a particular set of tasks.

For many women who have been stay-at-home wives and mothers, that moment may come when the children have gone off to college or have married and moved away from home.

For some people, the down time comes when a loved one dies or a long-term relationship of some type ends. The work the person has done for the other person—perhaps in twenty-four-hour-a-day caregiving or some other degree of responsibility—ends in some way.

In each of these situations, a person has allowed a job—a specific role, set of tasks, position, or title—to be a life. And that isn't at all what is supposed to happen. Life is comprised of a number of roles, tasks, and positions—and yet it is more than a composite of these things. Life is ultimately a set of relationships that we are to establish, grow, and nurture with others.

Out of a clear understanding of who we are—the talents and personality we have been given and the skills we have developed—we are to do the work that is put before us to do. That work has times and seasons; it comes and goes; it builds and grows. Our work is forever changing in some way, even as we have times and seasons, growth spurts, and an ongoing maturing and building up of ourselves.

Our work must not define us.

Out of the wellspring of who we are, we must define our work.

When we come to the still waters of life and we wisely use that opportunity, we are nearly always led to see ourselves in a new way.

Over a period of several months, I came to a far greater understanding of who Tim Lavender is as a man. I saw myself in a way I had never seen myself before.

Certainly in philosophy classes in college I had confronted the great questions of life: *Who am I? Where am I going? How will I get there?* I had confronted them as a young man in his twenties and—as wise as I thought I was at the time and as wise as any twenty-something person thinks he is at the time—my answers to those questions were at best partial answers. As a man approaching forty, I needed to confront those questions again. And I have no doubt about it: I will need to continue to confront those questions in every season of my life for as long as I live. We never fully answer the questions. But our understanding of the answers grows and grows and grows, the more we reflect on who we are, where we are going, and how we will get there.

A person does not need to be "made to lie down" or "be led to still waters" through a loss. I hope that this book will help you to see it doesn't take a tragedy, a major life change, or the loss of a loved one for us to say to ourselves, "I need to spend some time reflecting on who I am, where I am going, and how I will get there."

We can and should be intentional in pursuing a greater understanding of ourselves at all times, in all seasons of life. We should never allow the tasks or roles of our lives to become so all-consuming that we fail to do the inner work that we must do to become great.

I caution you, however, that this work cannot be accomplished in one evening of solitary staring into space or on one weekend retreat. You may begin the process in that way, but you aren't likely to end it there. Gaining an understanding of yourself rarely happens with one sip from a calm pool of water. Rather, you must enter a season of self-reflection and soul-searching. You must allow yourself the luxury of a season of less frenetic down time to do the work of the heart that can set you up for greater productivity and greater purpose down the line.

We all go through seasons in life. Springtime is for planting, for initiating new projects. Summer is certainly a time for production. Any person who grows anything knows that summer is a major season for growth, and ongoing, even tedious, work; it's the time when the hoeing and plowing and watering and weeding and fertilizing are especially intense. Harvest is the time for reaping the rewards of what has been produced. And winter?

Winter is the time for the land to lie fallow and to rest. It's the time when old wood is pruned away or old plants are uprooted and discarded. It's the time when the snows and rains turn any leftover foliage into mulch that benefits the soil. It's the time when the pests that can ruin a crop and plague the field hands are killed in sustained subfreezing temperatures—and at the same time, nutrients can be put back into the soil. It's the time for sharpening tools, sitting by the fire and staring idly into its flames, resting the body and mind and spirit, and as the months of winter pass, it's a time for planning the next crop year. All of these are wonderful analogies for our lives.

Winter for us is the season for allowing the "remains" of the immediate past to be uprooted and cleared away, and for plowing whatever is beneficial back into our lives.

Winter is the season for allowing time and space to do their work in sorting out relationships that help or hinder us.

Winter is the season for sharpening our skills, developing our innate talents, and giving ourselves time for reflection about who we are. It is the time to allow the creative energy within us to rebuild to the point that we feel ready, able, and eager to get out and plant something new with our lives.

Winter is a time for facing ourselves and for making a choice to be great in every area of our lives, including work but not exclusively limited to work.

You don't have to wait for a "winter" season to hit you to embark on the journey of self-discovery. Indeed, self-discovery is an ongoing process that you should pursue at all times.

Take time to stare into the still waters of your soul. Who do you see?

Others Will See and Follow

Others witness your response to adversity. When others see you exerting positive influence even in the midst of tragedy or adversity, they are much more likely to follow your lead.

Your willingness to explore the deepest recesses of your soul in down times, times of setback, or times of discouragement can lead you to discover areas of talent you may not have developed, to pursue skills you may not have acquired, to seek knowledge you may not have gained, and to explore areas of influence you may not have considered. The more you take time out to stare deeply into your well of dreams and talents, the more likely you will be to activate both into meaningful plans, useful skills, and positive influence.

The degree to which you actively seek to express your ideas, test your theories, sing your music, write your words, and live out your dreams will be the degree to which the inner you begins to exert influence on the world around you. *Bringing the inner you to bear on the outer world is influence.*

If you want to achieve personal greatness, embrace fully the challenges of life. Don't try to hide from adversity or sit down in the midst of it. Battle it, endure it, overcome it, and exert positive influence in the midst of it.

Don't dismiss the value of discovering more about yourself. Get to know the "real you."

Don't fail to express to the outer world the inner riches of your soul. Use your faith to give voice to what you believe and think and feel.

REACH INTO THE INVISIBLE WORLD

AS YOU MAY HAVE CONCLUDED FROM STATEMENTS I have made earlier in this book, the golf course became a special haven of peace and joy for me during my adolescence. It was also a place of learning a good many life lessons.

One particular incident that took place in my teenage years was a major turning point in my life. I was leading in a golf tournament and then made a few mistakes. In anger at my poor play, I threw my golf club up into a tree, and to my surprise, it came down in two pieces. My immediate thought was, *What have I done?!* I had done more than break a club that was valuable to me, not only in terms of dollars but also in terms of play. When a club is broken, it is declared to be out of play for the rest of the round. In other words, I could not borrow a replacement club in playing the remaining holes.

There were only a few holes left for me to play that day, but I lost the tournament. Not only had I blown my temper, but I had blown my victory.

As I put my remaining clubs in the back of the car later

that day, I heard a small voice speak deep within me: *You'll never become great unless you learn to control your anger.*

You may be saying, "Well, you were just a teenager. All teenage boys get angry from time to time."

The issue was deeper for me. I knew I needed to come to grips with the anger churning inside me. I knew it was time for my explosive anger to stop exploding!

That night I prayed and said to God, "I don't know how to get rid of this anger. But I want to. I need to. Please help me."

That was the first time in my conscious awareness that I made an effort to reach into the invisible world and ask my Creator to impart something of His character and His nature to me.

The invisible realm—the realm of God and all things of a genuine, positive spiritual nature—is far more vast and potent than our visible world. It is the realm in which we find all the things that we value most.

This morning, I reached into the invisible world and asked God to give me a spirit of forgiveness. I knew I would be dealing with a difficult situation and a difficult person in the hours ahead. I asked for compassion. And I also asked for wisdom and understanding about how to finish this chapter on the relationship between the invisible and the visible worlds in which we all live simultaneously.

Forgiveness . . . compassion . . . wisdom. These are intangibles, invisible "substances," and to some, ideas, concepts, or inner impulses. By whatever name you describe them, they are very real, very potent, and vital to our achieving personal greatness.

Your Relationship with the Invisible World

Your relationship with the invisible world is rooted in your relationship with God. I challenge you to take a look at that relationship today. How do you relate to God? Who is God to you? What do you believe God does for you—or doesn't do for you? What things are under His jurisdiction? What is the nature or quality of His actions on your behalf?

The way you respond to God and the way in which you receive things from the invisible realm is by faith. Faith is a believing or an inner knowing that the invisible realm exists, and that what we need most in life resides there.

The challenge we face is in knowing how to use faith to pull attributes from the invisible realm and manifest them in our practical daily lives.

What happened when I asked God to help me with my anger?

Almost immediately I was reminded of the advice, *Next time you feel angry, before you take any action, stop and mentally count to ten.*

That may have been something I had heard from my mother or a teacher or who knows where. But in that moment, I remembered that advice, and I believed it was the method for me to use when anger began to well up inside me. The next time I felt angry, I stopped and counted to ten. I did something in my anger, but it was something that did not bring harm to me, to others, or to a golf club. Counting to ten was a way of releasing the anger.

Please note that I wasn't suppressing or denying my

anger. To the contrary, I was recognizing it and expressing it, but in words, not deeds. Through the coming weeks, months, and years, I found myself counting to ten a great deal, yet it became less as the years went by. My anger was brought under control. And whether that was a mark of physical, emotional, or spiritual maturity, I do not know. What I do know is that I have never broken another golf club or had another angry outburst!

What Do You Need from the Invisible Realm?

I have a strong conviction that most of us know what we need from the invisible realm. We know our character faults and emotional weaknesses.

How do we come to this understanding of our flaws?

We discover our character faults through others telling us of them. Certainly this isn't the preferred way! Most of us find correction painful. We chafe under it.

I had an experience with this after I told a joke that I thought was funny. It wasn't lewd or racist. People laughed. But after the meeting in which I told the joke, a man I respect deeply said to me quietly, "Tim, your joke was a little offensive to me."

Everything in me wanted to reply, "You must be kidding!" I wanted to say, "Lighten up!"

Instead, I found myself saying, "Thank you for telling me that. I'll try to be more cautious about this in the future."

Did I enjoy that correction? No.

Did I correct my behavior? Yes.

In the vast majority of cases, those who identify our character faults do not act out of hatred or a spirit of confrontation. Rather, they act out of love for us—they desire for us to be all that they know we truly are or can be. Our pride keeps us from taking their gentle criticism to heart.

Apart from others telling us of our faults, *we have a conscience, and God has a way of pricking that conscience* when we engage in things that are harmful to us or to others.

We have been given the Bible, which I believe is the ultimate source of wisdom. It's ours for the reading. And the more we read the teachings of the Bible—especially the book of Proverbs and the teachings of Jesus in the Gospels—the more we are going to encounter principles related to character. These principles are going to take root in our minds as we read them repeatedly, and if we choose to remain sensitive to how God wants us to live, we are going to see a contrast between the things we do and the things we should do.

Let me give you an example.

Most of us live fairly self-centered lives. We become accustomed to being catered to, and if something we have come to count on happening doesn't happen for some reason, we get upset.

There is one thing that I know I need to do daily to keep from becoming self-absorbed or from becoming overly upset when people don't behave precisely as I believe they should behave. What is it? I know I need to be grateful for *everything* others do for me. The book of Proverbs tells me so. The New Testament tells me so. My conscience tells me so.

How do I pull this invisible trait of gratitude and

thanksgiving from the invisible realm? First, I ask God to help me show gratitude. I ask Him to prick my conscience at times when I need to say, "Thank you." I ask Him to make me genuinely thankful.

And then, I look for ways and times and people to whom I can say, "Thank you." I set my radar to scan for opportunities to say, "Thank you." For the cup of coffee that is brought to me, a copy of a document that is made for my benefit, a phone call that is returned, I choose to say, "Thank you."

I have discovered that the more I say, "Thank you," the more I am aware of ways in which others help me. I find more and more reasons to thank others! Also, I find it easier and easier to offer that thanks. In fact, saying, "Thank you," has become an automatic part of my response to virtually every act of kindness shown to me. And in the end, I am increasingly aware of the many ways in which God extends His kindness to me every day—through people, through circumstances, through intangible and tangible blessings. The more I thank other people and God, the more I feel thankfulness within.

Has thanking others become a habit? Yes. A good habit? Yes. A habit that has no meaning? Quite the contrary! Saying, "Thank you," is a habit that has taken on a great deal of meaning.

The Bible lists a number of traits that reside in the invisible world. Each trait is intended to be manifested in our behavior and speech in the visible realm. And each trait is something that God has promised in the Bible to provide to those who request them:

love	joy	peace
understanding	knowledge	discernment
wisdom	patience	kindness
humility	forgiveness	self-control
faithfulness	consistency	"right" responses
goodness	gentleness	compassion
health	diligence	energy
perseverance	strength	endurance
empathy	generosity	protection
provision	wholeness	courage
mercy	tenderness	creativity
hope	sensitivity	gratitude

This list is by no means definitive. I encourage you to add to this list based upon your desires and emotional needs. The question you must ask yourself is this: *Am I manifesting the good traits that I know I need to achieve personal greatness? If not, why not?*

The Bible says we have not because we ask not.

Make today the day you start asking the invisible God to impart to you the riches of His invisible realm.

NOT ONLY YOUR VALUES,
BUT HOW YOU VALUE VALUES!

The person who achieves personal greatness not only lives out of his sense of values, but also comes to *value* values. He recognizes that the things in the invisible realm are truly important.

In the end, what is money if you don't have integrity, family and friends, joy, assurance that you have a relationship with God, and all of the other intangibles that make life worth living?

What amount of status would you trade for good health?

What amount of fame would you trade for love?

We need to value intangible values before we will ever make the effort to reach into the invisible realm with our faith and begin to develop a character worthy of influencing others.

A friend of mine went to an auction and saw a mint-condition 1937 automobile being sold for $450,000. He had admired the beauty of the car as he surveyed the various items up for sale prior to the start of the auction, but he hadn't given any thought to buying the car. He certainly never thought it would go for that much money.

A year later, my friend was given the opportunity to purchase that very same automobile for $175,000. The owner had experienced financial difficulties and needed to liquidate some of his possessions quickly. My friend bought the car! He didn't know anything about its engine and he had never driven the car, but he knew its worth. He sent a down-payment check to the owner and then got on the phone to a person who he knew dealt in classic cars. Within a matter of days, he had sold the car for $275,000. Not a bad way to make $100,000 in a week!

What was the principle at work here? My friend had learned the value of the car.

How much do you value your relationship?

How much do you value your character?

How much do you value your life purpose?

How mudh do you value your personal greatness?

Your Potential Resides in the Invisible Realm

Your potential lies in the invisible realm as much as any character trait.

Your potential is not bound by a job or career, a bank account, a house with a three-car garage and three cars in it, a family and two pets, a few choice memberships, and a few favorite toys or hobbies. Your potential ultimately lies in the spiritual realm. And that realm is unlimited.

When we think about our potential, our natural inclination is to look to the material realm for a measuring stick. An investor is likely to look at his portfolio. A business executive is likely to look at the size of his company, his position on the corporate ladder, or his compensation package. A wife and mother is likely to look at the home she keeps and the children she is raising.

These measures are all concrete, tangible, and limited in capacity. The fact is, everything in the material world has a limited capacity. Hold a coffee cup in your hand, and you are holding something in the material world that likely holds six to sixteen ounces of liquid. Buildings can hold only so many employees; land can accommodate only so many buildings; an entire planet can have only so many square miles of land and water.

In sharp contrast, everything in the invisible realm has unlimited capacity. There is no end to the things that reside in that realm: knowledge, understanding, and wisdom can always be greater; creativity can always be greater; spiritual insight can always be greater; love can always be greater; faith and hope can always be greater.

One of the first principles that people learn in an economics course is the law of the scarcity of resources. Why isn't everything free? Because there isn't enough of certain items for everybody to have all they want of them. The scarcer a desired item, the higher the price of attaining it.

This law of economics that relates to the material world is 180 degrees opposite the law of the abundance of the invisible world.

Mercy and forgiveness are unlimited.

Love is unlimited.

Patience is described as being *long*-suffering.

Understanding and wisdom are infinite.

If we can begin to grasp the fact that we can tap into unlimited resources and begin to manifest them in a visible, practical, personal way, we are in a position to release our potential in the form of practical service and influence.

Let me give you an example.

There's nothing limited about having an attitude of forgiveness. Nothing puts a parameter or lid on our personal choice to forgive those who fail us, hurt us, reject us, or disappoint us. There is no scarcity of ability imparted to us to say to another person, "I will not judge you. I do not condemn you. Rather, I forgive you."

All things that are in the spiritual realm are unlimited.

When we choose to tap into the spiritual realm and claim the eternal qualities as part of our lives, and then choose to express them in practical ways on a daily basis, we move from scarcity to unlimited abundance in our lives.

The law of scarcity says there are only so many seeds in an apple.

The unlimited nature of the invisible world says there are unlimited apples that might grow as the result of planting just one apple seed, and then replanting some of the seeds produced in those apples, and then replanting some of those seeds, and so forth.

Virtually all scientific advancements begin with an idea—a hypothesis that exists only in the unseen realm. The strength of a hypothesis drives the focus of a scientific experiment, which exists in the tangible, visible realm. The result is the proof or disproof of a concept, and after a concept, procedure, or entity has been established, technology can then take over and give form and ultimately a product line to that concept.

Every song is first heard in the mind of a composer.

Every written word is first etched into the thoughts of an author.

Every harvest is first envisioned in the mind of a farmer.

Every redecorated environment is first seen in the mind's eye of an interior designer.

Nobody can see a thought, an idea, or a concept. It's in the unseen, immaterial world. But its manifestation eventually becomes tangible or material.

Reach into the invisible today. Ask for what you need to reach the next level in who you are to be. It is your warehouse for achieving personal greatness.

Live Life to Make a Point, Not a Profit

Years ago, a close friend of mine publicly shared the story of his father. He flew to his father's bedside just a matter of days before his father died. He was privileged to be with his dad at the very end. Shortly before his death, the father pulled his son close to his face and whispered these last words to him, "Live your life, son, to make a point, not a profit."

What potent words! I have never forgotten them. From the moment I heard them, they were emblazoned on my mind and my heart.

I knew this man who died. He had made a million and lost it, and remade it and lost it, and remade it. He was a World War II hero who managed to stay alive, even though the vast majority of his company of soldiers had been killed in combat. He was a fighter in spirit, with a strong drive to succeed and will to live. He had endured against great odds.

For the vast majority of his life this man had lived to turn a profit, and not only that, but to turn profit after profit into a small fortune. And yet at the very end of his life, he knew the greater truth: life is about making a point, not a profit.

Personal greatness lies in making a point—a positive, good, influential point of our choosing. Personal greatness lies in the way in which we live to make a point. It lies in the way we mold our talents into skills and then use our skills to influence others in a constructive, encouraging way.

WHAT'S THE POINT OF YOUR LIFE?

Michael Ellison is a close friend and associate of mine. As far as I am concerned, he has positively influenced more people around the world than any other single person I know. He has consulted with some of the largest and most far-reaching organizations in America, helping them to craft their messages and then get their messages out to the greatest number of people in the most effective, efficient, and timely manner possible. He is an expert in the use of print, mail, and broadcast media—he has taken some of the leading organizations today from virtual obscurity to worldwide influence. Michael has been a key behind-the-scenes, unsung hero for the spread of the gospel in the last half of the twentieth century.

I usually meet with Michael three or four times a year to go trout fishing at his ranch in Colorado. One year as we were preparing to pack and fly out of Phoenix, a huge snowstorm hit Colorado, and we had to cancel our trip. Michael said, "Let's just stay here in Phoenix and spend the day together. I'd like to share with you what's on my mind." Nothing could have pleased me more.

As we began talking, it became apparent that Michael had some questions about the direction he was moving in his life.

He was struggling inside to put all the pieces together regarding his work.

I said, "Michael, let's talk about your mission in life." I wrote out his life-purpose statement on a board in his office. For years, Michael had this as his mission statement: "Take the message of Jesus Christ through media ministry to the world." I knew very well what he considered to be the focus of his life.

At the time we were meeting, Michael had fairly recently launched a company named TriVita, which is a healthy living company devoted not only to physical health, but also to spiritual and emotional well-being. The name of the company literally means "three life"—implying life in the body, mind, and spirit. I had worked with Michael and his team to craft the mission statement, core values, promise, and public image for TriVita. I wrote the mission statement for TriVita on the other side of the board in his office.

"The two don't look as if they fit together," I said.

By the end of the day, Michael had reframed his personal mission statement to be this: "I exist to bring spiritual, physical, and emotional health and well-being to people." All of his media-related efforts fit well under that new umbrella statement. So did the purposes and goals of TriVita. Something unlocked in Michael that day—something that is still growing and is very good.

About a year later, Michael lost his largest account at the time—it was close to a $15-million-a-year account. I was concerned about how he might feel in the wake of that loss, so I went to see him. He said, "This is the most liberating thing that has happened to me in years. I have never felt better about anything in my life."

"Talk to me about that," I said.

He said, "A few months ago, I began to sense very strongly that I needed to devote myself full-time to TriVita. I didn't know how I was going to be able to do that. Now I know."

Within the next twelve months, Michael led TriVita to double in size to a significant company with a very powerful message. His energies were focused, his motivation was high, and his purpose was solid.

For years, I have worked with companies and individuals to help them frame their life-purpose statements, which are also called mission statements. Such a statement is basically the answer to a question each of us needs to ask, *Why do I exist?*

Can you answer that question in a single sentence? Does the answer cover all that you believe is part of your God-given reason for being?

As your potential expands—through the acquisition of information, the development of skills, and the exercise of your potential to exert positive influence on others—your life purpose is also likely to expand.

Don't back away from that. Revisit your life-purpose statement from time to time. Ask yourself again, *Why do I exist? Why am I here? What is the point of my life?* You may find that your life purpose has expanded as you have grown personally. In fact, expect it to expand!

IDENTIFYING YOUR TALENT COMBINATION

You have been gifted from birth in very definite, unique ways. You were born with a certain set of capacities, abilities, and talents. These inborn, inherent, innate abilities are fixed in you. They work together to create in you a one-of-a-kind talent combination.

Let me point out several things to you about your talents:

Talents Are Inborn Traits

You must discover and develop your inborn talents. You are born with an identifiable and fixed set of talents. Most people have three to five dominant talents, but everybody has at least one. These talents form the general framework of your potential for engaging in and successfully accomplishing certain tasks.

Talents Are What You Are Good at Doing

Your talents are the things that you are naturally good at doing. They are things you

- always seem to have had an ability to do, from your earliest memory;

- can do adeptly, almost from the first try;

- routinely achieve success in doing; and

- enjoy doing (because you succeed so often in doing them).

The things you are naturally good at doing are things about which you often wonder, "Why can't every person do this? It's so simple."

In my life, I recognize at least three of my natural talents:

1. Organizational skills. I have always been able to put the pieces of something together to make sense of the whole.

I have an ability to see the elements that comprise the whole and to see how they interrelate. Some of these skills might be defined as mechanical skills. My father had a natural ability to look at an automobile engine, determine what wasn't working, and fix it. I have this talent also—but I have applied my talent to see and solve problems of organizations.

2. Physical coordination. I am physically able to do and to repeat with consistency what I desire and learn to do physically. I have developed an excellent golf game in part because I enjoy golf immensely, but also in part because I am physically able to play the game well.

3. Visualization. I am able to see the end product, the final destination, and in the process, the various steps toward attaining that product or reaching that destination. I tend to see situations and organizations in terms of models and flow charts.

What are your talents? What have you always been good at? If you had any difficulty in coming up with five things you do well, I offer you this talent inventory from which to identify talents that may be built into you:

Organizational skills	Sense of humor
Musical talent	Artistic ability
Physical strength	Agility and flexibility
Eye-hand coordination	Athletic ability
Keen eyesight/hearing	Intelligence

Mechanical skills	Keen perception
Good memory	Social skills
Logic skills	Math skills
Verbal skills	A green thumb
Skill at oration	Creative writing ability
Ability to learn new languages easily	Ability to position items in pleasing ways
Boldness in trying new approaches	Strong interpersonal skills

Don't limit yourself to this list! Many other aptitudes, abilities, talents, and gifts exist. The challenge before you is to identify the talent combination that is uniquely *you*.

As helpful as it is to identify our talents, it is equally helpful to discern what we are *not* good at doing. Why? Because for every weakness or inherent "dislike" we have, there is likely to be a corresponding strength or inherent "like." It is helpful to know what is worth avoiding in life or where we are unwise to devote a great deal of time or energy. Each person is a mix of strengths and weaknesses; the goal, of course, is to play to our strengths and downplay or circumvent our weaknesses.

Years ago, I knew a young man who loved the idea of becoming a bass player in a rock band. He loved to listen to rock music and became quite knowledgeable not only about rock music but also about various rock bands. He had only one problem. He couldn't play the guitar. No matter how much he practiced, he couldn't master the instrument. The problem became more clearly defined the more he tried to become a guitarist: his fingers could not match what was in his head. He was a great listener, but a bad player!

Now, what does this have to do with strengths and weaknesses? The underlying aptitude related to rhythm is math. This young man had excellent math ability. The underlying aptitude related to tonality comes from the artistic side of the brain. This young man is not, never has been, and never will be artistic. Furthermore, he reflected that what he really enjoyed about guitar and rock music was that the bass guitar gave the driving beat for the group—it was the organizing factor. He also enjoyed the people-to-people aspects involved in putting together a band and scheduling performances.

His underlying talents were related to organization, people, "driving beats," and mathematical proportions. What wasn't this man going to be good at? Playing music, composing new music, singing, or copying music tediously offstage.

Where did this man find success in life? Not by playing in a rock band but by managing a rock band. He had what it took to take the show on the road—to pull together the right people in advertising, imaging, and transportation; to book the act into the right halls; to manage the money well; and to become the driving force behind the band's success. Musician? No. Business manager for musicians? Yes!

Dig deeper into your likes and dislikes. Does the idea of giving a speech put you on the path to apoplexy? Does adding up a series of numbers bore you silly? Do you seem to miss seeing certain things that others are quick to see? Define the underlying aptitudes or abilities for the things that seem to be your strengths and weaknesses.

Talents Are Your Domain of Success

Your success lies within your talent combination. For example, a person gifted with people skills and salesmanship may achieve a moderate amount of success in management, but his truly great success is going to occur when he pursues sales.

Comply, Don't Deny

You may attempt to deny your existing talents and abilities, but you can never replace your talents. It is not within any person's prerogative to decide that he wants a different set of talents. What you are born with is what you get. You cannot trade in one or more talents on other talents. You must use what God has given you.

Achieve True Fulfillment

You may let your talents and abilities remain dormant, but you will not experience true fulfillment in your life until you acknowledge them and pursue their development.

Talents are the things that you find easy and pleasurable to do, and that you have success in doing. They are the abilities that require the least exertion for success and give the greatest joy in accomplishment. At the same time, they are the abilities that you do not mind practicing or perfecting because the sheer joy of doing these things gives satisfaction.

What are your basic innate aptitudes, abilities, and gifts? What have you been good at for as long as you can remember? What kinds of activities and tasks have you found most enjoyable? In what areas have you found the greatest success?

A good friend once told me, "I've loved to build things since I was a little boy. For a long time I worked in construction as a project manager and, later, as a developer. I found great pleasure in seeing a building rise up out of the ground, take shape, and become a building of good design, on the inside and the outside. I began to understand that I am a builder. That's who I was created to be.

"When I understood that I am a builder by nature, I felt extremely liberated. I could build in any number of fields, in areas of people, service, and bricks and mortar. I found myself thinking, *I'm a builder, and because I'm a builder, I build. I build up my wife to be all she can be. I build up my children. I build up my family. I build up my employees. I build up my church. I build up every client for whom I do work.*

"Pursuing who I am gave me a great feeling of satisfaction—in fact, a far greater feeling of satisfaction than getting a construction job finished. I still build buildings and shopping centers and housing developments, but I build far more than that—I build up people."

Is this man leading a life that is fulfilling to him? Absolutely!

Is he complying with rather than denying his talents? Definitely!

Is he succeeding? Greatly!

THE LINK BETWEEN TALENTS AND SKILLS

Talents are things you have always been able to do, enjoy doing, and have success at doing. Talents are your capacities or potentialities, your inborn abilities.

Skills, in contrast, are the behaviors that you have developed to reflect your talent. For example, you may have an innate ability to organize information and communicate it to others. Specific teaching skills—such as how to construct curriculum, how to make valid and reliable tests, how to sequence information, how to create a lesson plan, and how to develop application exercises—are behaviors that must be learned, practiced, and perfected for a person to become an expert teacher.

Talents are inherent. Skills are learned or acquired.

Talents are the *what*. Skills can usually be defined in terms of *how to*. A physical strength and coordination talent might be expressed through acquiring martial-arts skills or developing the how-to skills related to lifting weights. An artistic or design talent might be expressed through developing drawing or interior decorating skills. The person with a talent for communication might develop the skills of how to give a speech.

Mozart was born with tremendous musical talent. He did not come out of the womb, however, completely proficient at playing the piano, composing music, conducting orchestras, or performing before the most powerful people of his day. He had to develop the skills related to his talent.

Having an ability to draw doesn't make you an architect. You need information and skills. Having the ability to sing doesn't qualify you for the starring role in an opera. You need training and experience and contacts. Having good large-muscle coordination doesn't automatically result in a professional sports career. You need coaching, physical training, and opponents to play against.

Name any talent and you'll soon recognize that there are corresponding sets of information that need to be learned, skills that need to be developed, and a great deal of practice that needs to be done.

Skills Are Learned

Every talent is related to information—historical, theoretical, practical, or concrete. We need to study, to learn, to experiment. We need to know more about what we have been equipped innately to do.

Skills Have a Practical, Tangible Component

Every talent is related to something tangible in the real world—an instrument or set of vocal cords, a golf club or football, a calculator or computer, a frying pan or a sewing machine, a vehicle or a piece of manufacturing equipment, a spreadsheet or a manuscript. The manipulation of these tangible entities, or the application of information and talent to these tangible entities, takes some degree of coaching and some degree of personal experimentation.

Skills Must Be Practiced

Practice is involved in developing any skill. You can learn all about a skill in theory, but that will not make you adept in the performance of that skill. Furthermore, practice never ends. Even people who have highly developed skills quickly discover that they need to continue to practice their skills to keep them sharp.

Ultimately turning a talent into a set of skills requires practice, practice, practice. No pianist ever gets beyond the need for routine practice of scales. No golfer ever gets beyond the need to go to the driving range or the putting green to hit a bucket of balls. No businessman ever gets beyond the need to go to a training course or a seminar to update his skills. No minister ever gets beyond the need to read and study the

Bible. No chef ever gets beyond the need to cook daily to keep culinary skills sharp. No physician ever gets beyond the need to read the latest medical journals or to practice medicine.

It is as we turn our dreams into plans and our talents into skills that our potential unfolds like a new horizon before us. Indeed, turning talents into skills is the prime way we leverage our potential and prepare ourselves for influential positive service to others.

THE LINK BETWEEN YOUR TALENTS AND PERSONALITY

Your talent combination is not the same thing as your personality. Personality tends to refer to qualities such as open/closed, high energy/low energy, laid-back/high-strung, bright-sunny/reflective-pensive, and so forth. In reality, many fairly closed (or shy), low-energy, and reflective personalities achieve great things! They may not be the most likely persons to win "Salesman of the Year" awards, but they just might win honors for "New Product Development" or "Best New Theory."

Your personality is the unique package—the wrapper—in which your talents are presented and your skills are manifested.

DON'T SHY AWAY FROM BEING A ROLE MODEL

Many people seem to shy away from the idea of personal greatness because they don't want to be in the spotlight. They don't want to have their actions or their character scrutinized. They don't want to face others' judgment.

The greater fact is this: you are going to be judged according to your character and works whether you want to be or not! Rather than try to dodge the responsibility of being a role model, why not embrace the concept?

I boarded an airplane recently and discovered that my stockbroker was also on the flight. We managed to trade seats so we could sit together, and as we traveled, he said, "I hear you're working on a book."

"Yes," I said. "I believe every person can learn to lead and every person can achieve personal greatness."

He said, "If I had a book with that concept today, I'd give it to every one of my clients and to every person who walks into my office."

"Why?" I asked.

"Because I encounter person after person who doesn't believe that he can become a leader or become great in the example he lives out to others. Most of the people I meet are hoping that they can become financially successful, but they see their personal lives as having very little impact on others."

I have observed the same attitude in many people who work for the organizations that have hired me as a consultant. The comment I hear, although it may be stated in slightly different terms, is this: "I'm not a role model." The subtext for that is: "Don't make me a role model."

In just the last couple of months, I have read two major magazine articles about popular personalities—one from the entertainment industry and the other from the sports world.

Both were quoted as saying, in essence, "I don't consider myself a role model to anybody. I'm not asking to be a role model. Don't call me a role model."

Why not? People who are in the public eye—especially to the degree these two people are—are going to be role models, whether they like it or not. They are going to exert influence on others, either positive or negative.

Why don't these individuals want to be role models? Is the reason that they don't believe in their character, their ability to exert positive influence, their integrity, their virtue, their "worthiness" to be followed or emulated? Are they just trying to appear modest? Are they trying to dodge the responsibility of their fame?

Their answers aren't as important to me as your answers about yourself. Are you willing to shoulder the responsibility that goes with your reputation? Are you willing to assume the task of being a role model? Are you seeking to live a life that others will want to follow? There's nothing prideful about saying, "Yes, I'm a role model. I want to be a good one." That's part of the territory that goes with exerting positive influence as you exercise your potential.

If you don't want to be a role model, don't seek fame.

If you don't want to be a role model, don't run for office.

If you don't want to be a role model, don't succeed.

If you don't want to be a role model, don't step up on a public platform.

If you don't want to be a role model, don't be a parent.

If you don't want to be a role model, don't open your mouth or be seen in public.

The point is: you *are* a role model for good or bad, for

somebody, at some point, in some situation or circumstance. It's unavoidable.

ACCEPT THE MANTLE OF INFLUENCE

If you are actively seeking to discover and pursue your potential, if you are turning your talents into finely honed skills, if you are producing excellent work and serving others in a way that is a positive influence, you are going to achieve personal greatness. The higher you rise, the greater your visibility. The greater your visibility, the more you are going to be evaluated according to the results you produce.

If you truly want to be your best and do your best, you need to accept the mantle of influence that will inevitably fall on your shoulders. Wear it graciously. Wear it humbly. Wear it in a way that brings honor to your life.

EMBRACE A LIFETIME OF LEARNING

WHEN I WAS A CHILD, I THOUGHT I'D BE A PHYSICIAN when I became an adult. I held on to that dream all the way to college. I was offered a physics scholarship to North Texas State, but I didn't want to study mechanical science. I was determined to pursue the life sciences, so I went to the University of Texas at Arlington, where I became a premed major.

After I had finished two years of college, my mother became disabled, and I felt I had to drop out to help support her. She was alone, and my younger brother was still in high school. I got a job, pursued a career in sales, and became very successful in business.

Then the day came when I was discussing an opportunity with my employer about heading a particular division of the organization. He said, "You really want to run this division, don't you?"

I replied with a simple but determined, "Yes, I really want to take this ball and run with it!"

He said, "All right. It's yours."

I became a little hesitant at that point and asked, "Do you think I have all the skills necessary?"

He became thoughtful as he answered, "No. You've got the brains and the street smarts and you've got the motivation and heart, but I don't think you have all the formal education you need."

That conversation took place on Thursday, and by the following Monday morning, I had enrolled at Dallas Baptist University. I worked all day, and then went to school at night for two years to finish my undergraduate degree. Two months after I finished my baccalaureate degree, I started an MBA program at Southern Methodist University, and two years later, I finished that degree.

My employer had been absolutely right. I learned a great deal that I found useful and practical in the years that followed, but even more, going back to school renewed my thirst for learning. That thirst has never been fully quenched. I am always in the process of studying something.

GETTING TO THE NEXT LEVEL

I cannot begin to tell you how many young men and women have come to me in the last decade and said, "I need to know more. Help me. Tell me where I should go and how I should acquire the information I need to know to move to the next level."

In many cases, the individual could benefit from formal training, which I consider to be training offered in a structured setting by credible and experienced instructors, in an accredited institution. If you are going to seek formal training, including a baccalaureate, master's, or doctoral degree, make sure you do so from the most experienced instructors you can find. Note that I used the word *experienced* regarding instructors. Choose instructors who are experienced as teachers and have had real-world experience in the field they are teaching. Such instructors are likely to be much more geared to practical application of theory.

Formal education very often places you in an organization in which you can learn more through experience. Without a doubt, experience is the most valuable teacher of all. But unless you are able to be in a position that affords you experience, you can't learn from experience. A formal degree is often the key that unlocks the door to entering a position that yields experience.

Many positions require degrees, certificates, licenses, or some other validation of credentials.

I worked with a young man, whom I'll call Don, who was involved in promotional work. He had a wonderful attitude, was a talented musician, loved to travel, and knew something about organizing concerts and events. He became the advance man who set up meetings and events for the leader of our organization. His work took him literally around the world.

One day Don and I were talking about his future, specifically his future in the organization. I said, "Don, I need for you to become a Certified Event Planner. You need to have that credential to gain the respect of those with whom you are working internationally, and in some cases, you need that degree to gain entrance to the offices of people with whom our CEO needs to work."

I knew Don hadn't finished high school, so he faced a double hurdle—finishing his General Equivalency Diploma (a GED is the equivalent of a high-school diploma) and then completing a Certified Event Planner course of study. I also told him that if he'd go on to college and get a degree, I'd find a way for the organization to pay his tuition.

Don initially took on the challenge. He completed the GED. But then he came to me and said, "I just can't continue. I'm not spending enough time with my wife and children, and I don't see how I can study and travel too." He gave up.

I eventually hired somebody to be Don's supervisor. She had a baccalaureate degree and Certified Event Planner credentials. She had what was required to help the organization move to another level in its seminar, conference, and event programming.

Jason was a different story. I found him in an organization working as a computer guy. I could tell he was talented in this area, but he had very little formal training. He had completed a junior college degree, but not a baccalaureate degree. I said to Jason one day, "You need to get your college degree in this area. What you learn will help us, but even more, it will help you."

Jason took on the challenge, and he completed the degree in almost record time. He stayed with the organization for several years, providing valuable assistance in building an in-house computer network back in the days when such networks were only beginning to appear in organizations. Then he launched out and started his own consulting company, and he has done very well.

Could he have succeeded without a college degree? To some extent, but I don't believe he could have gained entrance to some companies without a college degree. Of greater importance, what he learned in college was extremely valuable to him. He learned what was on the cutting edge of technology at that time, how to network with other professionals and how to avail himself of the resources necessary for him to stay on the cutting edge through the years.

"But," you may be saying, "the organization lost him."

The fact is, the organization gained a great deal from Jason's knowledge and experience in the years he was with them. Those in executive positions learned what they didn't know about computers, and they also caught a vision for the value of a good internal computer network. Jason, indeed, moved the organization to the next level.

The fact is also that Jason would have left the organization eventually. He had too much energy and was too smart to stay cooped up in that no-windows cubicle in the basement of a building, which is where I first found him. He might not have left to become a consultant or even to go to school, but he would have left because he would have felt bored and in a dead-end position.

There is always benefit to encouraging those around you to pursue more education—to be learning, growing, and developing as a person and as a professional. The benefits are tangible and intangible both to the organization and to the individual.

A MEANS OF GRAPPLING WITH CONSTANT CHANGE

Knowledge is multiplying at such an incredible rate in our world today that no person can truly be influential unless he pursues a lifestyle of learning. If you don't continue to grow and learn, pretty soon you will be out of touch—not only with information, but also with those around you whom you are seeking to influence positively.

Most people I know are not comfortable with rapid changes, yet we live in a rapidly changing environment. How do we cope with changes? How do we adapt to rapid change? By learning. By acquiring new skills, gaining new information, and growing in our understanding.

Learn in the Way Best Suited to You

What kind of "smart" are you? Every person tends to have at least one area of specific intelligence, and some people have two or three areas of specific intelligence, in addition to general intelligence aimed at acquiring, using, and remembering information.

Understand your learning style. Dr. Thomas Armstrong has identified several areas of intelligence: spatial, linguistic, interpersonal, musical, physical, intrapersonal, and logical-mathematical. Let me briefly summarize them for you:

Spatial intelligence involves thinking in images. Those gifted in this area can visualize details, draw or sketch their ideas graphically, visualize outcomes vividly, and orient themselves in three-dimensional environments with ease.

Linguistic intelligence involves the ability to argue, entertain, or teach effectively through the spoken word. Those gifted in this area usually read voraciously, can write clearly, and gain more meaning from print media than from spoken or visual media.

Interpersonal intelligence is the ability to understand and work with other people. It involves a capacity to respond to the moods, intentions, and desires of others and to "get inside the skin" of another person and see the world from his perspective.

Musical intelligence is related to a person's capacity to perceive, appreciate, and produce rhythms and melodies. Those with this type of intelligence usually have a good ear, can sing in tune, keep time to music, and discern different styles of music.

Physical intelligence is related to good tactile sensitivity, the need to move the body frequently, and physical coordination. Those with this type of intelligence often feel a gut instinct to act in a certain way.

Intrapersonal intelligence relates to one's inner self. Those with this type of intelligence are able to recognize and analyze their feelings, discriminate among their emotional responses, and guide their lives on the basis of their innermost desires.

Logical-mathematical intelligence involves the use of numbers and logic. Those gifted in this area have the ability to reason, put things in sequence, create hypotheses, see conceptual regularities and irregularities, and take notice of numerical patterns. They tend to be very rational people.

Knowing *how* you learn can be valuable when you need to acquire skills. You may be better at learning from tapes than books. You may learn best alone or in environments that involve interaction with others. As you pursue lifelong learning, make one of the subjects you study your own learning style!

Intuitive Learning

Not all learning, of course, is conscious. Not all learning involves the study of external sources of information. Some of the greatest lessons come from introspection; some of the most creative ideas come from intuitive impulses; some of the most important conclusions we draw are ones that we "feel" more than "think" in our spirits.

Very often some of the most profound insights come to us when we are not consciously studying. Very often the first thoughts we think upon awakening in the morning are creative and valuable thoughts. I can't begin to tell you how many times I have gone to bed at night mulling over a problem or issue in my life, and then find that I have the solution or answer upon awakening. It's as if our minds sort out our thoughts as we sleep, bringing us clarity on what have previously been muddled ideas and feelings.

Sometimes the thoughts that fly into our minds while we are taking a shower or soaking in a hot tub are thoughts worthy of further consideration. Be sensitive to the intuitive thoughts that spring to mind. Keep a notepad or dictation device within your grasp so you can capture the ideas for further reflection or study.

I have yet to meet a golfer who does not stand in awe of Tiger Woods. He has an amazing talent. Few people I encounter, however, understand that Tiger Woods is not only gifted physically as an athlete. He has two hidden attributes that have made him who he is: he is an incredibly hard worker, and he studies the game. Tiger Woods doesn't just show up at the start of a tournament after an all-night party and post below-par scores. Far from it!

First of all, I've never heard of any evidence that Tiger Woods parties. If anything, he has a reputation for having a life that is all work and no fun. He practices long, long hours.

He puts in his time on the practice putting green and at the driving range. And he studies the game strategically. He studies his swing and is always working to perfect it. Other people may think Tiger Woods has the perfect swing—but he himself doesn't think so. He knows that he doesn't hit every shot with perfection and that's his goal: to hit every shot perfectly.

Are you doing the work that it takes to get the job done *to the best of your ability?* Are you studying and learning new things that will help you do your job better? Are you learning from your experiences, taking the time to dissect and analyze your mistakes and successes to learn all you can about what to do and what not to do? Are you intentionally seeking to acquire the information that you believe will put you at the cutting edge of your career? Are you seeking the wisdom that is vital to the ongoing construction of solid business and personal relationships? Are you seeking out the wisdom that will result in your inner growth?

Purposeful Study

For the most part, learning requires purpose and discipline. Purpose and discipline are key elements of an exercise we call study. If you desire to learn, you must first set your mind to a specific purpose or area of study—a goal, a field to learn, a concept to master, an area in which to become informed. That area of study can change often. You may not seek to become an expert in one area as much as a fairly well-informed person in many areas. Generalists are just as valuable in our world today as specialists.

If you desire to learn something, you must also set aside time for study.

LEARNING IS VITAL TO
UNLOCKING POTENTIAL

Ongoing study and learning are vital to unlocking your potential, acquiring skills, and understanding how best to influence others.

Everybody wants a leader who knows what he is doing, where he is going, and how to negotiate pitfalls along the way.

Even more than knowledge, wisdom is required for influence to be effective and leadership to be consistently excellent.

Learn all you need to know to become all you desire to be and progress on the pathway of personal greatness.

Build a House of Trust

THE STORY IS TOLD OF FOUR SOPHOMORES WHO WERE taking an organic chemistry course at a major university. Each had done well on all the quizzes, midterm exams, and lab reports leading up to the final—so well, in fact, that they had A's going into the last week of the term. They were so confident of their success in the course that they decided to travel to visit friends for a major football weekend at a university in a neighboring state.

The four had a fabulous time with their friends, but after a long weekend of partying, they slept most of Sunday afternoon and decided to postpone their return trip to Monday morning. On the way back, they further decided that, given the fact they had put in no study time, they would be unwise to take the exam. They concocted a plan to meet their professor at the end of the exam period and explain that they had gone out of town for the weekend, had a flat tire on the way back, didn't have a spare, couldn't get help for a long time, and as a result, missed the final.

The professor heard their tale, and after a few moments of

thoughtful reflection, he agreed they could make up the final exam the following morning.

The students were elated and relieved. They studied diligently that night and went in the next day at the time the professor had designated. He handed each of them a test booklet, directed them to separate rooms, and told them to begin.

Each of the young men opened his booklet to find the first problem, worth five points, was a fairly simple problem about free radical formation. Each young man thought, *Cool! This is going to be easy.*

Each finished the first problem and turned the page. At the top of the second page they read: (For 95 points) Which tire?

SHOULD WE TELL THE TRUTH ALWAYS?

A person of greatness seeks to know the truth, including the truth of his potential, and then tells or expresses the truth.

Truth-telling sounds very simple, but it often isn't. Some major obstacles to telling the truth seem to be these:

- varying definitions for words;

- inconsistency in the message; and

- situational ethics.

Real truth is the foundation and core of all we believe. It is what we hold to be worth living and dying for. Without truth, we can never have lasting, rewarding relationships. We need, therefore, to confront these obstacles head-on.

Varying Definitions

To speak truth to a person, both you and the other person need to have a common understanding of definitions. Communication is in the mind of the recipient as much as it is in the mind of the sender of the message. Use words clearly and precisely. If you suspect that another person doesn't understand you, don't simply repeat what you have said. (And by the way, repeating what you said more loudly does *not* aid communication.) Ask the other person what he heard. Clarify your position if necessary until you reach agreement as to your message and its meaning.

Inconsistency in the Message

Don't say what you don't mean. Don't hedge—don't say one thing and mean another. Accurately and consistently state your message, and then restate it accurately and consistently.

One area of inconsistency lies between a person's head and heart. If you strongly believe you shouldn't say something, don't say it. Never go against what you believe to be the morally right thing to do. If you feel that one thing is right to say (usually the heart talking) but the other is expedient (usually the head talking), go with your heart.

Honesty is not only the best policy; it's the only policy to have.

Situational Ethics

Is it difficult to tell the truth in every situation? Yes. Is there a difference between telling everything you know and telling the truth? Of course. Is there a difference between volunteering basic information requested and volunteering all the details you know? Absolutely.

A person said to me recently, "We can never tell the truth all the time. If we did, we wouldn't have any friends. We would be telling people they are ugly and fat, and even though our words may be true, they would not be the right things to say."

I said, "Telling the truth is not telling everything you know. It is telling another person the truth that helps him become his best." We need to begin to distinguish between the ultimate truth and personal opinion.

Personal opinion is always rooted in limited perception, and it is always an expression of personal judgment. How do you know a person is ugly or fat? Who or what defines *ugly*? How fat is fat? What kinds of judgments are carried by those words?

In a number of organizations for which I have consulted, I have been asked to put together project teams and to hire people to fill key positions. Once I was interviewing a young man, and I explained to him that one of the nonnegotiable rules of the organization was to tell the truth all the time.

He said, "I don't think I can do that."

"Why not?" I asked.

"Life doesn't work that way," he said. "You can't tell the truth *all* the time."

"Give me an example of when you can't tell the truth."

He said, "If my secretary walks in and asks, 'Hey, how do you like my new dress?' and I think it's one of the ugliest dresses I've ever seen, I'm not going to tell her the truth. I'm probably going to tell her she looks great because I want her to do a good job as my secretary that day."

"You have confused opinion with truth," I said. "What you think about her dress is your opinion. Some opinions are better left unvoiced. And in most cases, you can state something that is not a lie, but still falls within the scope of an opinion. Truth is what can be substantiated, verified, backed up with facts, and holds to a rationale that is not swayed easily by opinions. Truth is rooted in values, principles, and key concepts."

Speaking the truth requires that we explore what leads to positive fruit, what motivates a person to excel and exercise his potential, and what builds up another person who has been emotionally wounded or psychologically disabled.

We need to speak genuine truth to others *always,* and we need to speak it to ourselves.

So what is genuine truth? Here are ten statements that are always true for all people in all situations.

- Unconditional love is a tremendous treasure that every person deserves to be given. Ask yourself, *Am I conveying the truth that every person deserves to be loved unconditionally?*

- Living free of guilt, sin, and shame is desirable for every person. Ask yourself, *Am I conveying a message that will help another person be set free from guilt, sin, and shame?*

- Evil exists, but so does good. Ask yourself, *Am I speaking truth that will lead a person away from evil and toward good?*

- Living in harmony with others is possible and desirable. Ask yourself, *Am I speaking words that promote peace and harmony?*

- Wholeness means to have all aspects of one's being—spirit, mind, and body—in balance and health. Ask yourself, *Am I conveying a message that promotes or encourages health and wholeness in another person's life?*

- Every person desires to have his material and emotional needs met. Ask yourself, *Am I speaking words that will help solve a problem or meet a need?*

- Excellence is always the best standard. Ask yourself, *Am I sending a message that inspires a person to do his best work or give his best effort?*

- Every person desires to have his broken heart mended. Ask yourself, *Am I speaking words that help heal damaged emotions and reconcile broken relationships?*

- Every person has a deep-core longing for God. Ask yourself, *Am I speaking words that help a person enter into a loving, satisfying relationship with God?*

- Every person desires to live in a way that brings him joy, satisfaction, and fulfillment. Ask yourself, *Am I conveying a message that produces joy and helps a person on the path toward satisfaction and fulfillment?*

A million compliments, words of encouragement, and statements of affirmation can flow from these ten simple and abiding truths.

Learn to see the heart, the motives, and the potential of a person. Learn to look for talents and abilities in a person. Focus on the character traits, values, and life purpose of another person.

If a person wearing an ugly dress asks you, "How do you like my new dress?" the greatest truth you can express may very well be, "Your dress is nothing compared to the beauty of your smile." You can find something to say that is rooted in truth and not a mere expression of your opinion.

These three principles should frame everything you say:

1. Speak what will produce good fruit in a person's life, in your life, and in the lives of those influenced by you and others.

2. Speak what builds up a person to value himself and to see himself as talented, intelligent, capable, and worthy of love.

3. Speak what motivates or energizes a person to develop talents and skills to the highest level.

HONEST, CANDID APPRAISALS

Truth-telling includes giving honest, candid appraisals and, when asked for them, expressing opinions in a straightforward and loving manner.

An acquaintance was hired back as a creative consultant to a firm she left a number of years ago. She walked into a meeting dealing with the firm's advertising and public relations, and those present asked her what she thought of the storyboards that lined the room. She took a quick look at the ad campaign being proposed and said, "This is terrible work."

She went on to provide an explanation to back up her opinion of "terrible," and then she gave positive and constructive advice on how to fix what she perceived to be an ill-conceived concept, poor wording, and outdated graphics.

Later she told a group of her friends, "I felt totally free to give my honest opinion, something I doubt I would have done ten years ago as an employee. When they asked me for my opinion, they got it—the whole truth and nothing but the truth from my perspective. I certainly made it known that I was giving them my opinion, but I also made no apologies that I am a professional in this field and that I had good, rational reasons for the opinions I voiced."

The group warmly received this woman's candor. The more the group responded to her opinions, the more it became apparent that all but one person in that room agreed with her assessment. Those present felt a new freedom to express themselves. A level of trust was established as each person stated his or her opinions candidly.

"And," this woman noted, "there was a fresh breath of creativity pumped into the room. It was as if somebody had opened a window to let out stale thinking. We had two hours of productive brainstorming, and by the end of the afternoon, we had the framework for a new campaign that was truly exciting."

As part of that discussion, those present also had to acknowledge to themselves and each other that they had thrown together the original campaign without sufficient thought or their best creative energy. This woman stated, "There was something of a secret vow—an unspoken but palpable commitment—to do a better job the next time around."

What emerged several weeks later was a campaign that had great impact on the public at large. And each person who participated in the campaign took satisfaction in knowing he had given the project his best effort.

Here's what telling the truth did in that situation, and what it tends to do in all situations:

- Truth challenges people to do what is noble, good, and right.

- Truth challenges people to give their best effort.

- Truth inspires a free flow of ideas, opinions, and emotional responses—all of which can be channeled into worthy tasks that are undertaken with maximum creative energy. In most cases, the creative free-flowing exchange of ideas results in projects, products, and services that are more innovative, more "on target" with consumer needs, and more influential in society as a whole.

Truth creates an atmosphere in which people are happier and morale is higher. The net result is generally increased productivity, greater efficiency, and lower rates of turnover.

When honest opinions or the honest truth is stifled, the exact opposite emerges:

- People do what is expedient or expected rather than what is the best or of highest virtue.

- People do the bare minimum required. They don't want to say anything more than what needs to be said to get a task done.

- Creativity is stifled, and therefore, projects, products, and services are less innovative and, in many cases, less effective and less influential.

- Group morale tends to be low and turnover high. The result to the organization is lower productivity, less efficiency, and generally a poorer bottom line.

Trust is the atmosphere in which people thrive. And trust is best established in an organization where honest, truth-based communication is free flowing in all directions.

When trust is demolished, a group suffers. Even if the group has only two people—for example, a marriage, a friendship, or a business partnership—trust is vital to the maintenance of a solid, growing, vibrant, enjoyable, and fruitful relationship.

WITHOUT TRUTHFULNESS YOU CAN NEVER BUILD TRUST

Any person who desires to be a genuine leader or to be personally great must tell the truth. Any person who desires to exercise his potential must be truthful to himself about his dreams and goals. He must be truthful in appraising opportunities and setting goals. He must be truthful in his relationships with other people if he is going to have a positive influence on their lives. It doesn't matter what the environment is; truth is required of all who seek personal greatness.

A person may be caught in a lie and continue to be an effective manager, supervisor, parent, teacher, attorney, or even president of the United States *for a time*. But that person cannot continue to be an effective leader over a long period of time without admitting the lie, seeking forgiveness for it, and changing his ways. There isn't enough parsing of words, justification of actions, or explaining away of circumstances to sidestep a blatant lie.

The inescapable fact is this: truthfulness is the foundation for trust.

How do you trust a spouse who doesn't tell the truth?

How do you trust an employee who doesn't tell the truth?

How do you trust an employer who doesn't tell the truth?

SHORT-TERM PAIN PERHAPS, BUT LONG-TERM BENEFIT ALWAYS

Not too long ago a man said to me, "When my son was sixteen, he got a serious speeding ticket. We went to court, and the judge asked him, 'Young man, are you guilty?' My sixteen-year-old said, 'Yes, Your Honor.' Then the judge said, 'Let me ask you again, but before you answer, understand this. If you say you are guilty, I have to take your driver's license away from you for a few months. If you say you are not guilty, then you will be entering a not-guilty plea, you will have the right to get an attorney and make a presentation in another court, and you may only have to pay a fine and not lose your license.'

"Well, at that, my son decided he wasn't guilty after all. Sure enough, he paid an attorney and a fine and kept his license.

"Was that the right thing?" this man asked—speaking to himself more than to me. "No," he concluded, "it wasn't the right thing. My son felt he learned that day that the law was not absolute and things could be twisted and purchased and consequences could be avoided. He made absolutely no change in the way he drove his car. He continued to speed. And the day came when his speeding resulted in a serious accident. He survived, but the people in the other car weren't as fortunate. My son lives with the guilt that he killed a mother and seriously injured her teenage son, who likely will be in a wheelchair or on crutches the rest of his life.

"Telling the truth would have been a more painful thing for my son in the short term of his life. Telling the truth was not only the right thing to do but also the more beneficial thing to do in the long term of my son's life."

You can't lie and have positive influence simultaneously. If you are truthful, however, you can overcome failures and mistakes and have positive influence.

The first step in virtually every recovery program is to say, "This is the truth about who I am and what I'm doing." Nobody is perfect—we are all works in progress—but we can all admit our faults, address them, and seek to overcome them with our disciplined and diligent effort and the help of supportive family and friends.

I have no doubt that tens of thousands of man-hours a year are spent in covering up mistakes in the workplace. Thousands more hours are spent in writing self-justifying memos and having explanation-laden appointments. Hundreds of thousands of man-hours a year are spent in uncovering mistakes that were denied and rectifying them, often at huge expense. No organization can survive very long if lies, innuendos, and attitudes of denial are allowed to run rampant.

The sooner an error is recognized and admitted, the sooner it can be addressed and corrected.

I've seen it happen again and again: a person who lies is forgiven by the people who matter the most to him if he admits the lie and asks forgiveness for having lied. He may lose his job, but he will gain the respect of those who can help him the most for the rest of his life.

Do the Right Thing *Always*

A client said to me in light of a negative incident in his company, "I'm not sure how we are going to deal with this particular situation because it isn't in our handbook."

The truth is, most of life isn't in *any* handbook—at least not in a specific, prescriptive formula to enact.

What most people do have, however, is a pretty good sense of what is right and wrong. We even say to ourselves that an idea "rings true" or a plan "sounds right," even if we can't point to a specific precedent or section of the bylaws.

If you have any doubt about the right thing to do, ask a person with good values and a reputation for integrity. Seek wisdom from wise people.

The right thing is not always spelled out in black and white. Sometimes it is etched on the heart.

You Already Know the Right Things

A man and his girlfriend asked me to give them counsel about how to resolve a problem in their relationship. I listened to them at length. I watched how they interacted with each other as each told his or her side of the story. I listened to them until they had fully vented their feelings and opinions, and they finally said to me, "What do you think?"

I said, "Ted, stop being rude to Christine. Quit using swear words. Be kind to her. Speak kindly in her presence."

I said to Christine, "Stop lying. Stop exaggerating. Stop making excuses that you think will justify your lying."

Profound counsel?

Not at all. Ted and Christine could have told me that it's wrong to be rude, to swear, or to be unkind. They could have told me that lying and exaggerating (a form of lying) are wrong. They just didn't see in themselves the very simple facts of their behavior.

Most negative situations aren't all that complicated. Not ultimately. They may have messy components, detours, and layers of self-justification, but ultimately the basics of right and wrong behavior are pretty plain and pretty simple.

Do the right thing.

Love other people.

Don't lie. Don't commit murder. Don't covet what other people have. Don't allow yourself to act out of envy or greed.

Don't be unfaithful.

Do work hard and give your best to every effort. Don't be lazy or slothful.

Do keep your anger in check—aim your anger toward constructive and positive expressions of solving problems.

Honor and respect other people, and especially have respect for all those in authority over you—at home, on the job, in the community, and in the church.

Own up to your sins, and seek forgiveness for them. Apologize when you make a mistake or hurt someone.

Take responsibility for your actions.

The list goes on. You already know the right things to do. Stop making excuses for not doing the right thing and choose to do what's right. Build a house of trust and you will become great.

LEARNING TO DO THE RIGHT THING

Many people seem to have an intuitive sense of right and wrong. In all likelihood, however, these intuitions were learned in very early childhood as their parents taught them right from wrong. If you have any question about whether you are doing the right thing, ask someone who has a record of showing that he knows right from wrong.

To know what is right or wrong is one thing—to do it is another. Action always speaks volumes more than intention.

Remember four main points:

1. *Think about what you choose to do.* Don't just wander through life doing what seems to come naturally. Much of human nature is prone to greed, lust, and a desire for fame or power. Be deliberate in your chosen course of action.

2. *Learn to frame the issue or situation that is immediately at hand.* Define it. Confine it. Refine it. Before a question can be answered, it first must be asked.

Learn to ask the right questions. Then in answering the right questions, make sure you have adequate and accurate definitions.

Limit the issue—give parameters to it. Every meeting cannot be about every argument. Every conversation cannot be about every topic. Every argument cannot be about every problem that has ever existed since the beginning of a relationship. As you begin to discuss an issue or pursue a solution, refine your position to involve even more accurate definitions, more precise plans, and more effective and efficient procedures.

Thinking this way involves focusing your time and effort. Choose to do what is most important and to work toward accomplishing immediate goals that you see in the context of the desired longer-range results.

3. *Grasp all options.* Most problems have more than one solution, and each solution tends to have multiple facets. As you weigh options, one is likely to emerge as the best option for you and others involved in that circumstance at that time. Don't get into a rut of resolving all problems in the same way, or approaching all relationships with the same mind-set. Allow for variations.

4. *Always act in a way that is consistent with your values and principles.* Ultimately the solutions, decisions, and actions that are going to work well for you are in line with your values, beliefs, and principles. Get to the core of the principle associated with each option as you pon-

der an issue, decision, or solution. Is it ultimately a matter of honesty, efficiency, effectiveness, morality, fairness, sensory satisfaction, quality, or personal profit? After viewing an issue or decision through the lens of principle, the "right" decision usually becomes clear.

AT THE CORE OF INFLUENCE

Doing the right thing is central to your having influence on others.

Your values, life purpose, and guiding principles all work together to direct what type of influence you seek to have on others as well as how you will grow in your influence and what you will do in times that you fail to live up to your expectations.

A person with noble values is going to seek to engage in noble service.

A person with a strong life purpose is going to be highly motivated.

A person who has firm guiding principles is going to be diligent.

And a person of noble, motivated, focused, and diligent service is going to be a strong leader!

ROOT RELATIONSHIPS IN TRUST

My son, Jacob, and I enjoy pheasant hunting. We have gone several times to a place in southeastern Kansas that has a lodge named Show Me Birds.

One year I returned from an exhausting business trip late the night before we were to drive from our home, which was in Arkansas at that time, to this hunting paradise. I said to Jacob at 4:30 that morning, "I am so tired. Would you drive this morning so I can get an extra hour or so of sleep? If you'll drive up there this morning, I'll drive back this evening."

Now from the time Jacob was a child, he has always found it very easy to fall asleep in a car. In fact, if Jacob was crying as a baby, Joy and I discovered that the surefire way to stop him from crying—the one method that worked if all others failed—was to buckle him into his car seat and go for a drive. We wouldn't get all the way around the block before he'd be sound asleep. There's something about the hum of the road and the motion of the car that causes him to nod off almost immediately.

The remembrance of those times flashed through my mind as we got into the car. I asked as I began to recline in the front passenger seat, "Jacob, can you stay awake?"

He said, "Dad, you can trust me. I will stay awake."

I fell asleep almost immediately and awoke about an hour and a half later feeling much more refreshed and ready for a day of tramping through the fields of Kansas.

On the way back home, Jacob admitted, "Dad, I can't begin to describe to you how sleepy I began to feel this morning. I was fighting sleep with everything in me. Every time I began to think, *I'm not going to be able to do this,* I would think, *I promised Dad. He trusted me to do this. I told him I wouldn't let him down.* And in remembering what I said to you, I would suddenly feel more alert."

I trusted Jacob with my life that morning—literally. He responded to my trust by trusting more in himself to do what he said he would do. He not only added to my trust in him, but he also added to his trust in himself to make a promise and keep it.

CREATING TRUST IN OTHERS

How does a leader generate trust in those he is influencing? Here are several ways trust is built:

- Create energy by making and keeping active promises, which are promises made out of your will and desire rather than promises made in reaction to problems or mistakes.

- Show your commitment to others by constructing mutual agreements that are beneficial to all concerned.

- Demonstrate character by doing what is right in the moment of choice—walking the walk and not just talking the talk.

- Confirm your relationships by revisiting your agreements often—remembering the past, recognizing the present, and reinforcing the future.

- Display competency by developing the expertise necessary to deliver your part to the relationship—recognizing that expertise is the result of education plus experience.

- Be consistent and predictable in your actions.

- Take time to communicate clearly and regularly.

- Be quick to listen first, talk second; communicate difficult news in person. Pass negatives up the corporate ladder and positives down.

- Create an emotional connection; sincerely care about others, and act from your heart to show respect, bolster value and equity, and impart dignity to others.

Trustworthiness is the one character trait that allows the other traits of leadership to exist. Without trustworthiness, giving and receiving falter.

Without trustworthiness, influence cannot function fully and tends to give way to control or manipulation.

Without trust at work in a relationship, adversity can destroy that relationship.

Without trustworthiness, a person is not likely to remain committed to the potential of others.

Without trustworthiness, what a person learns and the ways in which a person grows can lead to unrestrained uses of power.

Without trustworthiness, the balance a leader seeks in his life cannot be maintained over decades because family relationships and friendships will disintegrate into brokenness.

TRUST IS BUILT OVER TIME

After three months of thoroughly reviewing the organization of a major client, I sat down with the CEO of that organization and said, "Here's what I have learned about your organization. Here's what I recommend to do. And here's how I recommend that you proceed in getting those things done."

He said, "I want the results you have outlined, but I'm not sure I understand the implementation procedures you are recommending."

I said, "Perhaps we should implement the plan one step at a time, stopping to evaluate the overall results at the end of each step."

He was comfortable with that approach, and we began to implement the reorganization plan we had outlined to accomplish very specific end results. It took two years to rebuild his organization so that it was maximally flexible, quick to respond to market needs, and postured to handle rapid growth. The company began to run so smoothly on an international scale that this CEO felt he needed to make only about one call a week to his chief operating officer. He spent the rest of his time working on new products and establishing new markets to keep the organization growing and at the cutting edge in its field.

What happened in those two years was not only the remaking of an organization, but also the building of tremendous trust. When a series of observable and testable results are found to be worthy, the risks of making further changes are perceived in an entirely new light—the light of trust. We trust those who have proven themselves trustworthy.

Don't expect to build trust overnight. The process takes time. It often means tackling one part of a plan at a time, not engaging in a major overhaul in one fell swoop.

This principle applies to virtually all relationships. Marriages are not built in a day, and they are not rebuilt or renewed in a day. Friendships are not built in a day. The relationship between a pastor and his parishioners, a professional service provider and a client, is not established in a day.

You cannot declare a new day of trust in a relationship and instantly brush away all that is past. Trust is initially built step-by-step, and if trust has been breached, then the rebuilding of trust is again a step-by-step process.

Throughout my career, I have traveled a great deal. For virtually all of my marriage—which has just passed twenty-five years—I have probably been away from home nearly as many days as I have been at home. Yet never once in all that time has my wife, Joy, asked me, "Were you faithful to me while you were away?" It would not be an unfair question to ask. But Joy knows me. She knows the depth of my commitment to her and to our marriage and family. She knows who I am.

And conversely I have never asked her, "Were you faithful to me while I was away?" I know her. I know the kind of person she is. I know the depth of her commitment to me and to our marriage and family. And we both know the commitment that each of us has to our faith and to living by God's commandments.

Travel is an inconvenience, and not always enjoyable for either of us, but it is not a threat to our marriage. Faithfulness and trust are the foundation of our life together.

TRUST IS RELATED TO CLEAR COMMUNICATION

The most successful leaders I know are also the most skilled communicators. They know how to relate to their audience, even if that audience is one other person in a conversation. They know how to put their message into succinct, clear language. They know how to express themselves with passion and power, yet not come across as being overly emotional.

A person with a doctorate in communication told me that effective communication occurs when you know for sure that the person to whom you are talking got your point. It's not enough for a person to understand clearly the words you speak; the person must also understand the meaning of those words in the context of his life.

I have since found that definition of *communication* incomplete. Effective communication occurs not only when you know a person has understood your point, but also when you know how what you said makes him or her feel. See the difference? That way you know your words have entered the heart and mind.

Communicate Honestly and from the Heart

Telling the truth is inescapably linked to your ability to be an effective communicator. People can perceive that you aren't telling the truth if you aren't accurate in the way you express your beliefs, opinions, or even factual content.

They will also believe that you may be hedging on the truth if you aren't passionate about what you believe. It doesn't really matter whether or not your presentation style is polished. People will stop and listen to what you have to say if you have a passion for something and are attempting to convey your passion in an embracing and open way.

Benjamin Franklin was on his way to hear a well-known preacher when he was stopped by someone who said to him, in essence, "Why are you going to hear him? You don't believe a word he says."

Franklin responded, "But he does."

Before you can effectively communicate the truth, you

must be convinced that it is the truth and you have a passionate belief that others need to hear what is true. The stronger your conviction about something, and the more strongly you feel that others need to become informed, enlightened, inspired, or instructed about your conviction, the more strongly you will feel motivated to do your very best at communicating your message. Messages from those who truly are passionate in what they believe, and intent on communicating their belief passionately, are the messages we remember most clearly.

Invite Feedback for Clarification

One day I walked into an organization that had hired me as a consultant, and I said, "Take me to the area where your complaint mail is processed." I found one of the most antiquated, slow, cumbersome processes I have ever encountered. Customer service is so vital to an organization that I had to ask, "*Why* are you handling the mail this way?" The woman in charge of the area said to me, "The president of the organization told us to answer the complaint mail personally and warmly, just as if he were answering it."

This woman had interpreted the president's statement to mean that complaint letters needed to have handwritten responses. That wasn't at all what the president of the organization meant!

Be careful how you interpret a person's directives, admonitions, or evaluative comments. You may not have fully understood that person's intent.

Many people seem to internalize rejection and criticism when none was intended. They harbor bitterness and anger for essentially no reason other than their insecurity.

If you believe someone has wronged you, get to the core issue. Did you perceive the situation accurately? Ask questions of the person. Find a point of resolution. And ultimately come to the point where you can forgive that person. Let go of the anger and bitterness. Find common ground on which to build, or rebuild, your relationship.

If you believe someone has misunderstood you, invite feedback for clarification. Does he understand your instructions correctly? Does he understand the procedures required and the level of quality expected? Ask for feedback until you are certain the person understands what you are conveying. Be patient. What you say is not always what is heard.

BELIEVE FOR THE BEST IN OTHERS

A significant part of establishing trust is believing for the best in others—the best character, the best values, the best intentions, the best behavior, the best attitude.

After I had worked with one client for several years, the CEO accused someone of sabotaging the company's reputation by planting lies about the company. This person was stunned and emotionally crushed by the accusation. He was devastated that his integrity was being dealt such a blow, and he came to me for advice.

He asked me questions like, "How can I trust a CEO who so easily falls prey to lies?" "Why did this man choose to believe one set of lies put forth by one man rather than believe the validity of my work over time?" He felt that the trust he had worked so hard to build over several years of faithful, quality service had been undervalued and perhaps had never been truly recognized or acknowledged.

He was dealing with powerful emotions. He was concluding that the CEO was far more insecure, suspicious, and untrusting than he had ever realized. After all, if a person automatically chooses to believe the worst about someone rather than believe the best about him, where is the trust? If a person automatically chooses to believe a lie rather than pursue a rational exploration of the truth, where is the trust?

I encouraged him to do two things: 1) Slow down and wait for a few days, and 2) walk toward these allegations in all truthfulness. In the end, he emerged the truth-teller and his integrity was validated. (Someone else had initiated the rumor that impugned his character.) It took hard work to rebuild that relationship because trust had been broken.

My advice to those who seek personal greatness is this:

Be careful whom you accuse, lest you accuse them falsely.

Don't automatically accept anything that is said negatively about another person. Get the facts.

Don't assume the worst about a person. Believe for the best.

AVOID SLANDER AND GOSSIP

Be very careful in what you say about others who are not present at the time you speak. Nothing can destroy trust quite as readily as your gaining a reputation for speaking ill of others who have no opportunity to defend themselves or justify their actions.

Don't talk about other people in a negative way. The result

is not only a ding in the other person's reputation, but also a ding in your own reputation.

Don't speak about yourself in negative terms. Don't call yourself "dumb," "stupid," "clumsy," "inept," or "bad." Nobody truly aspires to be those things, so don't adopt the labels for yourself. You just may convince yourself that you are unlovable, unworthy, and incapable of success. And if others overhear you berate yourself, you may convince them that you are speaking the truth of your character.

Don't gossip. Gossip is the telling of partial truths to further one's own purposes. Face your intent in trying to tear another person down. Note your less-than-noble motives. And recognize that you can never know the full truth about another person. At best, you are telling something that you consider to be true from your perspective. You are engaging in conjecture with the intent of building yourself up through the tearing down of another person. Don't stoop to such poor character.

Trust Is a Must

Keep in mind always that for a person to receive your influence, he must believe that your motives are good and that you are trustworthy. Once trust is broken, it is difficult to mend. Choose instead to guard trust carefully and to do your utmost to avoid breaking trust.

It doesn't matter how great your talent, how well developed your skills, how intense your effort to help others, you simply cannot influence those who don't trust you. You cannot become great without a strong foundation of trust.

SEEK TO INFLUENCE RATHER THAN CONTROL

ONE OF THE QUESTIONS I FREQUENTLY ASK MY CLIENTS is this: "How many people do you truly believe you can control?" If a person is honest, he's probably going to come up with a number ranging from zero to one. The only person you can truly control is yourself.

Every husband knows that, even if he desires to do so, he cannot control what his wife thinks, says, or does.

Every employer must admit that, as much as he may try to do so, he cannot absolutely control what his employees think, say, or do.

Every teacher faces the challenge daily that, no matter what he may say to try to control a classroom environment or learning outcomes, he cannot absolutely control what his students think, say, or do.

If we cannot control, what can we do? We can influence others. Which brings us back to square one. Influence is the way we lead. Manipulation, control, and a mandatory or dictatorial approach are all dead ends in the long run. What you manipulate you ultimately drive away. What you control you kill. What you mandate becomes the focus of rebellion. What you dictate becomes an obstacle in the path toward greater quality, effectiveness, and efficiency.

Many executives are of the opinion that the greater the control they exert over an organization, the more work will be accomplished. The reality is far different. The greater the control from the top down in an organization, the less others give their best effort, ideas, or enthusiasm to the work they do.

The Creator created mankind with a free will. The laws and commandments He issued were parameters with consequences, but they were not control mechanisms. Mankind has the free will to stay within the parameters of moral and ethical behavior, or to stray beyond the parameters and suffer negative consequences.

Manipulation Versus Control

Manipulation and control are two different things. When a person realizes he cannot control others—in other words, he cannot force them to think and act in the exact ways he desires—he often resorts to manipulation, which is the establishment of external rewards and punishments to push others toward acting a certain way. Manipulation very often plays to feelings of guilt, inadequacy, low self-worth, or weakness in another person. It is using the weakness a person already feels to push him toward doing something that promises to make him feel stronger, more accepted, or more worthy.

How does influence differ from control or manipulation?

Influence recognizes that every person is a free moral agent. It takes the approach, "I'm going to do what I can to speak truth to this person, to help this person, to do the right thing by this person, and to challenge this person to pursue his potential to a level of excellence. I'm going to make myself available to this person in whatever way he wants me to be available. And then I'm going to trust this person to make his own choices and decisions."

Influence is relationship-oriented—as opposed to outcome-oriented—when it comes to another person's moral character and free will. Influence is concerned with the success pursued and achieved by the other person. Influence takes the position, "What can I do for *you?*" rather than, "What can you do for *me?*"

Influence to a great extent is exerted by example, not by rules or dictates. Influence points a person in what is perceived to be a good and beneficial direction, but it does not shove the person to pursue that direction.

Time and time again I find top executives in organizations who spend more time trying to control or manipulate the actions of individual subordinates than they spend in guiding the company as a whole toward greater market relevance, greater growth, greater innovation, or an improved bottom line. When an executive spends more time trying to control the behaviors of his employees than establishing the vision or building the strategies that inspire creativity, efficiency, improved quality, and greater effectiveness, the company suffers.

In some cases, I believe people find themselves at the top of the corporate ladder without sufficient management training. They assume that it is the "job" of a CEO to tell other people what to do, how to do it, and when to do it. As a result, they issue directives that say, in essence, "Do this, and when you finish that, come back and report to me. Then I'll tell you what to do next."

The far better approach is to say, "Here's the goal. Here's the end result I want to see. Give me a general plan for how you intend to accomplish that, and let's make sure we are in agreement on your methodology. Then go get the job done." The person who seeks to influence and who is intoxicated with the success of others is going to say to those beneath him on the organizational ladder:

- "I trust you to do what you say you are committed to doing."

- "I trust you to be loyal to this company and to do your best to build up this company."

- "I believe in your creativity, your skills, and your intelligence. I want you to be innovative and compassionate and excited about getting the job accomplished."

- "I want to help you in any way I can to help those under your supervision to produce maximum quality, with great effectiveness and efficiency."

- "You know your people. Let's work together to generate exciting ways to motivate them and reward them."

- "You know more about doing your specific job than I know about it. Tell me areas where productive line performance can be improved, where weaknesses can be strengthened, and where gaps need to be filled in."

- "I value your initiative and your effort. Let's agree upon a series of steps that are logical, deadlines that are reasonable, and an allocation of resources that is affordable."

- "I give you authority over those you supervise, even as I hold you accountable for their performance. But I also authorize you to be a compassionate leader who seeks the best for your subordinates."

- "I value the ambition you have for greater success in your life, and I want you to help me help you to release even more of your potential."

- "I ask you to help me set goals for your area of responsibility that are challenging and that will help the company grow and gain greater market share."

ATTACH PEOPLE TO RESULTS, NOT TASKS

If you build an organization that assigns tasks to people, then the more tasks your organization acquires in the process of growth, the more people you are going to need to do those tasks. People begin to be perceived in terms of their "labor," as hands needed for tasks rather than as people with potential.

In contrast, if you build an organization that is aimed at attaching people to results, then you allow employees to exercise their potential in determining how and when and what is necessary to best attain those results. There is a release of their creativity, skills, and energy toward accomplishing a goal.

Certainly, broad parameters should be established for how a person pursues the goal, but the details need to be left to the person.

An executive who is intent on assigning tasks to individuals is never going to see maximum energy or results from his company, or his area within a company. The executive who agrees with his subordinates on specific goals and procedural guidelines and then turns them loose to reach those goals using their own initiative, energy, and creativity is far more likely to see his company grow, excel, and develop an atmosphere with superlative morale.

I have yet to meet a person who does not respond to the challenge of a people-attached-to-results environment. At the outset, some may be suspect. Along the way, some may stumble and fail to reach the results they thought they could achieve. But overall, the model is an extremely strong one that produces amazing results for the vast majority of individuals and organizations.

On the flip side, I have never met a person with a high degree of skill, initiative, creativity, and energy who responded well to a tasks-attached-to-people environment. Such individuals feel stifled—as if they are in a cage.

What tends to keep an organization from moving from a tasks-attached-to-people environment to a people-attached-to-results environment? One hindrance is an executive who is insecure and who does not trust those he hires to work for him. Such executives fail to see that, in the long run, they are shooting themselves in the feet—they are hiring only those who will be willing to "do as they are told." They will be hiring less than the best—employees who have less intelligence, less motivation, less ingenuity, less energy—and in so doing, they will never achieve the full greatness for their organization that they desire.

Can an insecure, untrusting executive become a secure, trusting one? It's tough. A person who is accustomed to holding the reins tightly is going to be reluctant to let go. Such a person needs to recognize that the reins are never completely out of his hand, and that releasing the tight hold can and should happen incrementally as results are achieved and trust is established.

I never advise an executive to suddenly allow total decision-making freedom to an employee who has been held tightly in check and who has been functioning in a task-oriented environment. Rather, I advise that the executive begin to work with his immediate subordinates to solicit their input and to reach agreement on goals in one area under their authority and on general guidelines for procedures. Then he trusts the subordinates to pursue the results, exercising their discretion as to how the goal is to be reached, when subgoals or sections of the goal are to be reached, and who is assigned to the goal.

Your Influence As a Parent

Let me be very practical as a father for a moment. Parents are responsible for their children's physical, moral, educational, and spiritual welfare. Because they have that responsibility, they also have the authority to insist that their children obey their rules as long as the children live in their home or are dependent upon them legally and financially. Every parent dictates behavior to a child to some degree. But long-standing influence that a parent has over a child is not couched in terms of family rules.

Influence is exerted by example, by training up a child in the way "he should go"—a way in keeping with the child's potential, not the parent's potential. It is exerted by helping a child discover his God-given talents and by helping a child develop skills that are in keeping with those talents. It is exerted by helping a child find positive ways of aiding other people, learning from others, and ministering to others—in other words, it is helping a child find avenues to express positive influence.

Influence is exerted by spending time in the presence of a child and allowing that child to look through an open window into your heart—to learn how you do what you do, how you feel about what you do, and why you feel compelled to do what you do.

A child who believes he has been positively influenced is a child who loves to follow a parent long into adulthood.

A child who believes he has been manipulated or controlled by a parent is a child who forever seeks to escape and rebel against the parent's wishes.

You as a parent have a right to control certain aspects of your child's behavior, but you have a far greater privilege: influencing your child to want to keep the commandments and follow the rules that you know are best for him.

EXERTING POSITIVE INFLUENCE

One day I was wandering along Fisherman's Wharf with a client. We were in San Francisco on business but had a day off between appointments, so we took advantage of the opportunity to have some fresh seafood and, afterward, some ice cream. As we stood in line at the ice cream vendor's stand, I felt a tug on my shirt, and I turned around to find myself face-to-face with a homeless man. The man asked me as he pointed to my client, "Is that who I think it is?" He gave me the accurate name of my client.

I said, "Yes. How do you know him?"

He said, "I see him every Saturday night on television at the mission where I sleep. Do you think I could meet him?"

I said, "Absolutely," and I had the privilege of introducing this man to my client.

My client talked to this man for fifteen minutes. I had no doubt that it was a life-changing encounter for both of them. Not only had the man benefited from my client's teachings for several months, but he had experienced a direct and personal interaction with a television "hero." It was a powerful moment for him.

I drew two personal conclusions from that San Francisco encounter:

1. *Personal encounters are important.* What you do "live and in the flesh" is always going to be the most potent expression of who you are. It isn't enough to call or write or send tapes or show up in E-mail. "Face time" is always vital to deep and lasting influence.

2. *Variations in expenditures of time and energy may be necessary.* The amount of time required to have genuine influence in another person's life varies greatly.

   It does not take much time or energy to exert influence in some relationships. In other relationships, it takes a lifetime of sustained energy and focus to exert influence. Never assume that if you speak or act once, your message has been heard, your message has been internalized, or your message of influence has hit home in such a way that the person will act differently because of it. Always assume that you need to go back to the person again and again to do as much as you can.

Influence As a Choice

Influence cannot be mandated. We cannot force our influence on others. We cannot make another person receive our message, believe as we believe, follow in our footsteps, or emulate our characters. That is true for parents as well as business leaders, for pastors as well as friends.

Positive influence is voluntary, both on the part of the influencer and on the part of the person being influenced. The influence exerted by a great person doesn't require obeisance, honor, or servitude from others. It allows those who are being influenced the privilege of free will—it allows them to choose to be influenced or not.

Sustaining Positive Influence

Influence must be sustained if it is truly to be positive. You cannot be positive one time and negative another and come out on the positive side. If anything, negative influence outweighs positive influence. It takes far more effort to build and sustain a good reputation of integrity and high moral character than it does to destroy such a reputation. One act can take a person down in flames of infamy.

I have met many people through the years who have had awesome potential, but they were unable to sustain positive influence on others. They stopped pursuing and developing their talents, or they stopped using those talents in a positive way to benefit others. Choose to have positive encounters and to sustain your positive influence over years and decades.

HELP OTHERS DEVELOP THEIR POTENTIAL

I have a friend who loves to keep a tight rein on people. He once asked me to meet with a member of his staff to "find out what's going on with him." He wanted to know this man's goals and aspirations. This staff member and I couldn't meet immediately because he was getting ready to leave for an international trip so I asked him to take some time on his long flights to write down his personal goals and what he hoped to become and to accomplish in his life.

I received a document from this man that was one of the most honest and compelling statements I have ever read. I could tell he had really poured his heart into what he stated as his dreams and goals.

My client also got a copy of the document, and he said to me shortly thereafter: "I disagree with your methodology on this. You are creating disillusionment in people."

I said, "How is that?"

He replied, "When you ask people to state their goals and aspirations, you are causing people to think that they can achieve things in their lives that they probably can't achieve. When they fail, they will be disillusioned."

I said, "I don't believe that by refusing to address dreams and desires, we help people unlock, explore, or pursue their potential. It is only when a person feels he has freedom to exercise his potential that any organization gets the best from that person. There's nothing to gain by suppressing the truth of a person's dreams and goals."

My friend said, "Well, what if I lose this person now that he has faced his dreams and desires? What if he decides to leave my organization because he realizes he can't accomplish his goals working for me?"

My response: "So? What's your point? You'd lose him eventually anyway. You gain nothing by trying to stifle him, change his dreams, or thwart the pursuit of his potential. Perhaps the real energy should be directed toward finding ways the organization can encourage this talented and motivated young man to pursue his dreams and desires within the broader context of this organization's goals."

My friend asked, "Are you saying I should change the goals of this organization to appease this one person?"

"Not at all," I said. "What I'm saying is this: you have a very talented employee here. He's eager to help you. He admires and appreciates and enjoys working for this company. Consider him a valuable asset, and make room for his talents. If possible, put him in an area that challenges his innate dreams and desires. Find a niche in which he can grow and give 110 percent. You don't have to change the goals of your entire organization, but you may have to adjust a job description or two. If you don't, you'll lose this man within a few years, and at that point, the loss to you will be greater than the loss to him."

It is only when a person has a genuine "I-care-about-other-people-as-much-as-I-care-about-myself" attitude that the person gains our respect and admiration to the point we are not only willing but eager to be like him and follow his example.

BECOME INTOXICATED WITH THE SUCCESS OF OTHERS

Those who feel they must control the actions of others are insecure about themselves. In fact, the *more* a person seeks to control another person, the *less* secure he is in his worth and ability.

Those who are controlling or manipulative are the opposite of those who are intoxicated with the success of others.

I use that word *intoxicated* because for me, the greatest high in life is in helping other people succeed. I find tremendous pleasure and excitement in seeing those I love or value do their best and exercise their potential.

The joy I feel in seeing my daughter, Rachel, succeed in college and in life is exhilarating. She is already one of the greatest people I know. Surely all parents must feel that way when they see their children begin to move into their potential, succeed at what they desire to accomplish, and exhibit the character they as parents had desired so much to see manifested in them!

My delight is to see others do as well as I am doing and to see others do as well as they can do—which may very well be far beyond the success I am myself experiencing.

A person once said to me, "Being intoxicated with the success of others takes tremendous generosity of spirit."

So be it. A generous spirit is a hallmark of personal greatness. Those who are stingy or self-focused, or who are reluctant to express their praise and appreciation for others, rarely are considered to be great leaders.

You can't be intoxicated with alcohol and function normally. You can't be intoxicated with drugs and function normally.

But you can be intoxicated with the potential of other people and function at a supernormal level—a level that is better than normal.

My friend Dr. Scott Conard recently said to me, "I think my life is about developing the potential of other people." Scott is a medical doctor with about fifteen thousand patients—he has ten physicians working with him to care for them. He could just as easily have said to me, "My life is about building my practice, running my business, becoming rich and famous, and writing books on health and medical issues." Instead, he said to me, "I'm driven by the desire to see people get well and stay well. I'm driven by the desire to see other people develop their full health potential."

I have no doubt that's one of the reasons Scott has fifteen thousand patients. Who wouldn't want a physician with that as a life purpose?

No matter what career field you call your own, you can become intoxicated with a desire to see other people pursue their potential and become the best they can be.

THE HEART OF A SERVANT

Those who are intoxicated with the success of others are those who have a servant's heart. Being a servant means helping others to build themselves up and to achieve what they desire to achieve. Being a servant means letting others dictate the agenda for their lives, and doing your best to help them carry out that agenda.

Being a servant is the opposite of using people. It's letting people use you to the extent that you willingly offer your wisdom, your expertise, your skills, and your time, energy, and talents to assist them. It does not mean being abused by others, but it does mean making yourself available to them to help them move forward in their lives.

Jesus taught that those who are great are the ones who first are true servants. He said, "He who is greatest among you shall be your servant" (Matt. 23:11).

When we truly humble ourselves, walk away from pride, and give ourselves to helping others succeed, we are rewarded with a life of purpose and deep inner satisfaction. Further, we achieve an even greater level of greatness and influence.

This model of developing leadership goes against the grain of the vast majority of leadership models in the world today. It goes against the way society as a whole thinks and operates. Nevertheless, it is the ultimate model for becoming great.

Help others find their dreams.

Help others identify their goals and make their plans.

Help others develop personal relationships and networks.

Help others build practical skills that can turn dreams and plans into reality.

Help others discover avenues for positive influence.

That's being a servant.

And in helping others, you are exerting positive influence in their lives, and you are becoming a leader. People want to be influenced by someone who is truly on their side and has their best interests at heart.

If you want to lead, first serve.

HARNESS THE POWER OF RECIPROCITY

I HEARD SOMEONE JUST THE OTHER DAY REPEAT THE AGE-old proverb: "What goes around, comes around." I hadn't heard that in a while, but it reminded me of one of the greatest laws I have ever learned in my life: the law of sowing and reaping.

I grew up in a single-parent home. My mother worked hard as a receptionist to put food on the table for my brother and me. She did a great job of providing for us, and I learned many wonderful life lessons from her. One of the lessons was generosity—Mom had a big heart and very freely gave to those who had even less than we had.

From my mother, I inherited a propensity to give to others. I can't remember her ever sitting down with me to teach me about giving. Giving was something I "caught" from Mom. Many lessons in life are like that. They aren't taught, but caught.

Another old proverb says, "The more you give away, the more you receive." This seems to be the opposite of what makes rational sense. If a person wants more, then he should hold on to what he has, not give it away—right? Wrong. I also learned from Mom that the more we gave the more we received.

For years, I gave. Then came a day in my life when I had no more to give. Through a chain of events and poor decisions, I found myself penniless and at the point of bankruptcy. I felt devastated inside and struggled to understand how I had arrived at that point of near financial disaster. Even then, however, I knew that the principle of sowing and reaping was a law of God—I call it the law of reciprocity. I knew that law applied to everyone, in every place, for all time. I knew it applied to me. I just didn't know *how*.

One day when I was at my lowest—I was selling golf balls I had won in tournaments just to buy groceries for my family—a dear friend called. While we talked, his words warmed my heart. A few days later, as I was opening the mail, I found an envelope from this friend among the bills. In the envelope were an encouraging note and a five-hundred-dollar check.

I couldn't believe it! And there's no way I can adequately convey what that check meant to me in that hour. The money was much needed—I immediately handed it to my wife, and she headed for the grocery store.

Far more than the money, however, that check unlocked something inside me. It opened my heart to hope and love and value and appreciation and God's providential care. It reminded me of the law of reciprocity. It reminded me of the principle of sowing and reaping. It released something inside me that freed me instantly. It reminded me that I had a storehouse in heaven into which I could tap. Suddenly I remembered all the "seeds" I had sown in my life.

That night in my prayers I reminded the Lord that I had been a giver—that I had sown good seeds and I needed a good harvest.

I will spare you the details, but let it suffice to say that within the next year, new people almost miraculously crossed my path, and doors of opportunity swung open for me. Within twelve months, I had paid every bill I owed and I was totally out of debt! The harvest didn't stop there. Over the next several years, I reaped a harvest that can only be described as abundant.

I still give. I still receive. The law of reciprocity is real, and it applies to your money, your time, your investment in people, and any other thing you are able to sow or give.

GIVING AND RECEIVING

My friend Michael has one of the finest business minds I have ever encountered. He has spent his life building companies that bring great value to clients around the world. He literally has given his life for others in order to have a positive influence on them. Without a doubt, he is one of the greatest givers I have ever met.

There was a time, however, when all Michael did was give.

As a matter of fact, he felt very uncomfortable when members of his staff or his friends would send him a birthday card or gift. I find it hard to relate to a person being uncomfortable at receiving a gift on his birthday—I've never had that problem. In spite of my knowledge of Michael's reluctance and discomfort in this area, I did some research, found something I knew he would enjoy, and sent it to him.

Shortly thereafter, I received a phone call.

"What do you think you're doing?" the voice asked.

"Michael, my dear friend, how are you? Happy birthday!" I said.

"Tim, you know how uncomfortable receiving gifts makes me," Michael said in a very serious tone of voice.

"Yes, I know, Michael, but let me ask you a question: How do you feel when you give someone else a gift?"

"Awesome. I feel as if giving is one of the things I am privileged to do and talented at doing. I feel very satisfied and happy when I have an opportunity to give to others," Michael replied.

"That's wonderful," I said. "I can tell that giving is a special talent you have and that it makes you feel as if you are serving your life's purpose to give. But guess what? I feel exactly the same way when I give to others. As a matter of fact, I think most people feel really good about giving to others.

"So, here's the problem, Michael. If you are only a giver, then you are denying people around you who care about you the same joy and fulfillment of giving that you feel. And you are denying them that joy for one reason."

"What's that?" he asked.

"You are a terrible receiver. You don't understand that the law of reciprocity is the law of giving *and* receiving. It's not just the law of giving. You are robbing me and others of the joy we'd like to experience in giving to you."

Michael grew very quiet. I think he was in shock. He said to me, "I have never thought of it like that."

Giving is not a one-way street. To develop ourselves as leaders, we need to embrace the entire principle: giving *and* receiving.

Today Michael is a changed man. He still remains a great

giver. But now he has come to see that his giving is a seed that grows in the lives of others, and therefore, he must be able to receive some of the fruit of that seed back into his life.

Not Only a Matter of Material Goods

A person of greatness comes to understand that giving and receiving are not limited to money or material goods. Much of our giving and receiving has nothing to do with tangible goods or services. Giving and receiving often occur in conversations. We receive what another person wants to share—from pain to joy—with not only a listening ear, but also a caring heart. We give out of our experience—from pain to joy—with a compassionate voice and an eye toward encouraging the other person or helping the other person with practical advice and illustrations. In doing this, we give and receive genuine friendship.

A generous heart overflows in all areas of giving: time spent together, service, presence in times of need, prayer, assistance in carrying emotional and spiritual burdens. The rewards that come to a generous giver are often things that money cannot buy: love, health, opportunity, new ideas, friendship.

A woman shared with me that she had enjoyed almost a six-hour conversation with a high school friend she hadn't seen in nearly thirty years. This friend had written a note in the aftermath of their long evening of sharing. The note read, in part: "In spite of all you've been through, you have maintained your faith, and you have persevered with a joyful heart. I wanna be like you." My friend said, "That was one of the greatest compliments I've ever received."

This woman had been an inspiration and a positive influence on a classmate from long ago because she had listened, had shared from her heart, and had opened herself up to a giving-and-receiving encounter that occurred at a deep level.

A giving-and-receiving conversation is

- a two-way street. No one person dominates the conversation.

- personal. Both persons are willing to share information that is personal.

- emotionally involving. Both parties are willing to take a risk in sharing information that gets to the deep issues of life.

- filled with questions and answers. Both parties are willing to ask questions and give answers—fully, honestly, candidly, and without a hidden agenda.

GIVING AND RECEIVING APOLOGIES

One of the greatest things that you can give to others is an apology when you have erred or failed to act. An apology is always warranted when you realize you have left something important undone or unsaid.

I worked with an organization for a couple of years, and then the day came when I faced a philosophical difference that I could not bridge between myself and the CEO. It wasn't a moral issue, but a difference in perspective on how an organization should be run effectively and efficiently. I was asked to execute a strategy in which I didn't believe, so I resigned.

My exit from that organization turned out to be much more negative than it should have been—flat out, I did a poor job in leaving. I had deep regrets about our parting of ways, but frankly I didn't seek to remedy the hurt feelings between the CEO and myself. I left a number of things undone and unsaid in my parting.

At the start of the year 2000, I reached into the invisible world and prayed, "God, somehow, in some way, I want to make things right with this man." I didn't call or write, but I felt a peace that, indeed, somehow and in some way, this would happen.

About eleven months later, I was returning from a business appointment, and my connecting flight was canceled. I was put on the next available flight. As I boarded the plane and sat down, I heard a voice say, "Not only did you steal my best employee, but now you've stolen my seat!" I looked up to see this man grinning at me.

I asked, "Are you sitting right here?" as I pointed to the seat next to me, which was the only empty seat in that area of the plane. He sat down, and I immediately said, "This is a God event."

He said, "I believe that. I wasn't even supposed to be on this flight—my flight was canceled."

We had come from different directions and had intended to take different connecting flights, both of which had been canceled, and there we were, sitting next to each other. Nobody but God could have figured that out.

As we took off, I said, "I want to talk to you about the things I know I did wrong in the way we parted. I also want to hear from you about the things you think I did wrong. And no matter what those things are—the things I know and the things you tell me—I want to tell you I'm sorry about the way our relationship ended."

We had an awesome conversation for the next two and a half hours. We mutually forgave each other, and just as important to me, I was finally able to forgive myself and move beyond the guilt I had felt from that experience. When I got off that plane, I felt as if God had given me an early Christmas present.

Not only is it vital that you apologize for things you have done and left undone, but it is also important that you are quick to receive an apology offered by someone else. Be a generous receiver in this area. Accept the apology offered to you, and then let go of the issue to which it is related. Don't hold on to resentment or ill feelings. Release them!

It has been a tough lesson for me through the years to learn to forgive quickly or to accept apologies sincerely and immediately. For many years, I tended to hold on to hurts too long, including the memories of ways in which I hurt myself. I held on to guilt too long—even after I had asked God for forgiveness.

What I have recognized in most truly great people, however, is that they are quick to ask for forgiveness, they are quick to offer apologies and to accept apologies sincerely and readily, and they are quick to forgive themselves, release any guilt they feel, and move on.

GIVERS INFLUENCE GIVING IN OTHERS

Giving and receiving friendship is vital to your influence. What you give influences others to become good givers.

What you receive with an open and thankful heart influences others to become good receivers.

Greatness requires us to be open to others: to receive what others offer, and to give what we have to give from the riches of our inner selves. The greater our generosity in giving and receiving, the greater our opportunity to lead and exert influence. An ability to give and receive is vital for personal greatness.

DEVELOP A KNOCKOUT PUNCH

EVERY BOXER KNOWS THAT A GOOD KNOCKOUT PUNCH is essential. Generally it's a one-two punch that's quick and delivered with power.

In personal leadership, we should be quick to deliver that one-two punch, and deliver it out of great inner strength. It is a punch that does not hurt—rather, it gives joy and freedom to the other person. It is a punch that brings about change, and generally it puts an end to conflict. It knocks out anger, hatred, bitterness, and feelings of revenge.

This attitudinal knockout punch is (1) gratitude and (2) forgiveness.

AN ATTITUDE OF GRATITUDE

When my children were young, they'd often moan at something I'd tell them to do: "Aw, Dad, do we have to?"

"No," I'd respond. "You *get* to."

I said that so many times that it almost became a family slogan. My children finally got to the point where they'd look at each other after I'd given them chores to do and say, "Looks like we *get* to do this."

Be grateful for the things you *get* to do each day.

The person who is on oxygen in a hospital critical-care unit would love to be able to have the energy and health to rake your leaves.

The person who is begging for food in the street gutter of a major Third World city would love to have your garbage to take out.

The person who has only a cup of rice as food for the entire day would love to have the privilege of cooking dinner for your family.

The person who puts in sixteen hours a day behind an ox in a hot, humid rice paddy would love to take the elevator to your air-conditioned job on the fortieth floor.

The person who walks three miles over an unpaved path to get to a school would love to wait five minutes at the gas station to pump gasoline into his SUV.

Be grateful for the place you live, the car you drive, the job you have, the family and friends you have, the church in which you are involved, and the opportunities you have to enjoy recreation, the arts, sporting events, and movies with popcorn at the local theater.

Be grateful that you have the opportunity to lead your life—to discover your talents, develop skills related to them, and influence others.

Developing a Thankful Heart

Not too long ago my wife, Joy, and I built a new home. In many ways, it is our dream home. One day I left the construction site and started grumbling about a subcontractor who hadn't done the right thing and hadn't shown up at the appointed time for me to discuss the mistake with him. Suddenly I came to my senses. I thought, *How fortunate I am to be building this home! How many people in the world get to be involved in the design and construction of the place they live? How many people ever get to build their dream home? Tim, be grateful for what you are doing here. Focus on the big picture of this, not on the mistake of one subcontractor.*

I took control of my attitude that day and changed it. I developed an attitude of gratitude about my house, and as a result, I've enjoyed that house far more than if I had moved into it with a grumbling, complaining attitude.

Complaining is contagious. You may think, *Well, I'm just blowing off steam. I'm not hurting anybody by voicing my complaints and criticisms.* The fact is, you are hurting yourself. You are wasting precious time and energy by focusing on the negative. The deeper you dig a hole of negativity, the longer it will take you to climb out of that hole and begin to function positively.

Voicing your negativity does affect others, especially those who are closest to you. They may not even hear anything you say, but they'll feel your attitude and sense your mood. Your negativity is likely to cause feelings of insecurity, volatility, and negativity in others. Choose instead to have a positive influence.

You will encounter a thousand things every day that are worthy of your thankfulness, from small to great, tangible to intangible, interpersonal to highly personal, national to local, spiritual to material. Focus on the good things that are happening to you, around you, in you, and through you.

Voice your thanksgiving to God. I heartily recommend that you start your day by voicing your thanks to God that you have another day in which to live and work and love and praise and extend God's blessings to others. End your day by voicing your thanks to God that you have lived successfully through another day and that you have been able to work and love others in a way you hope and believe will bring honor to His name.

Voice your thanksgiving to others who bless your life—from the postal carrier who brings a package to your door to the janitor who empties your trash at the office.

Voice your thanksgiving to third parties. Express your thanksgiving for your child's teacher not only to the teacher but also to your child, to the principal, to the superintendent, and to other parents.

Choosing to Confront All Negative Attitudes

Confronting and uprooting negative attitudes is one of the most difficult things many people do in their lives. It takes intentional effort to say, "Hey, my life is not about criticism. It's about building positive values and principles and engaging in positive activities that yield positive influence. I need to stop being rude, selfish, angry, cynical, and critical. I have a higher purpose than that!"

Choose to reengineer your speech. Even if you don't feel positive, speak positive words to yourself and others.

"But," you may say, "isn't that hypocritical?"

No, not if your ultimate intent in life is to become a more positive person.

You have programmed yourself to think negative thoughts and voice negative words to the point that these thoughts and words have become habitual. You need to reengineer your mind and speech toward a new habit, a new positive expression. To do that, you need to hear yourself, with your own two ears, speak positive words. Those words trigger positive thoughts, which in turn will eventually create a thought bank for producing positive words.

An attitude may have an emotional component to it, but it is not pure emotion. It also is part will and part idea. In speaking positive words with your will, you are voicing a positive idea. The emotions related to a positive will and positive idea will eventually follow. And in the end, what you want to say will be what you say, and what you say and do will be what you feel. There's nothing hypocritical about that!

Your attitudes dictate behavior. Positive attitudes generally produce positive behaviors. Negative attitudes generally produce negative behaviors. Therefore, the nature of your influence—positive or negative—begins with attitude.

Our Great Need to Forgive

I recently read an article in *Forbes* about the first CEO of AT&T. He was asked what he considered to be the foremost leadership trait. He said, "That's easy. It's forgiveness. To be a great leader, you must learn how to forgive."

Forgiveness is a matter of the will. It is a choice. Even if you don't feel like forgiving, you can and must forgive. Furthermore, forgiveness is not only a matter of forgiving in your mind—releasing a person from your inner hatred or vengeful thoughts. It is not only saying that you forgive.

Genuine forgiveness is acting every day, in every way, as if the person is forgiven.

Many people are confused about what forgiveness is and isn't. Let me offer an explanation.

What Forgiveness Is Not

Forgiveness does not mean that you deny the pain you feel. Neither does it mean that you do not want justice to right a wrong. Forgiveness is not saying, "It doesn't matter, it didn't hurt, or it hasn't affected me." Rather, forgiveness is a willful process of saying, "I will not be shackled by what you have done or said, or have failed to do or say. I will trust God to deal with you, and I will trust God to help me let go of the hurt I feel and to recover from the harm done to me."

As much as we need to forgive others, we also need to forgive ourselves and to seek forgiveness from others. Rarely is any situation totally one-sided. In most cases of hurt, pain, or rejection, two persons are involved in varying degrees and in varying ways.

The Three Phases of Forgiveness

There are three phases of forgiveness:

1. *Admit it*. Own up to the fact that you have been wronged or that you have committed a wrong.

It's easy to see how others wrong us. It's much harder to see how we may have harmed others. The truly mature leader will recognize the need to forgive as well as the need to ask for forgiveness.

Beyond what others do to us, or what we do to others, another area that often goes unexplored is our inner response to what we or others have done. We need to admit that we have been hurt by what has happened, or that we have guilt for having hurt others. We need to own up to ourselves that we are harboring ill will or anger, or that we are feeling rejection, bitterness, or hatred.

It is only as we openly acknowledge our feelings that we can begin to be set free from their negative consequences in our lives. And believe me, deeply held feelings of anger, bitterness, or hatred bring nothing good to a person in the long run. When these emotions take deep root in a person, they produce a wide variety of emotional and physical diseases— and in turn, they wreak havoc with a person's professional and personal lives.

Face a hurtful situation fully—what you did, what the other person did, and all of the feelings related to the situation. Admit that a wrong has been committed.

Above all, admit the wrong—and the emotions that go with it—to God. Admit to God that you have messed up and feel guilty about it, or that you are feeling sad or mad that others have wronged you. Admit to God that you desire justice, healing, and forgiveness. And then go to the person you have wronged and apologize. Seek to make whatever amends are appropriate.

One of the most vivid examples of asking for forgiveness that I have ever personally experienced occurred in the first two days of a new job I had a number of years ago.

Actually the organization was not a new one to me. I had been involved in one division of the organization, but then the CEO of that organization decided to switch executives. He put a man who was in an executive position into a slot in the division in which I had been working, and he asked me to leave the division I was in and take this man's position. In essence, the two of us were exchanging jobs. I was in full agreement with the wisdom of that decision and accepted the challenge wholeheartedly.

What I did not realize in making this change, however, was that this man's staff had been very loyal to him and advance rumors had not been very favorable toward me.

This man's secretary—who was now to be my secretary— and several others in the office were ice cold to me on my first day in the new position. The next morning, the secretary, Donna, asked if she could meet with me privately. I agreed, thinking she was probably going to submit her resignation.

Instead, this is what she said: "Everybody in this office was told that you are purely focused on business and that you are a cold, matter-of-fact person. For weeks, we've been dreading your coming. After one day of working with you, however, I realize that none of that is true. I have already apologized to my husband for thinking ill of you, and I want to apologize to you for the way I behaved toward you yesterday and for misjudging you in advance of knowing you."

What a bold move that was on her part! It was a move I've never forgotten. Donna has been my secretary, apart from a few brief timeouts here and there for personal reasons on her part or mine, ever since that day. She has been the epitome of a faithful, loyal, steadfast, highly skilled, competent, very warm employee and friend.

All of us are going to have points of moral or character failure. We're going to have the day when we say or do something that we know is contrary to what we desire in our heart of hearts to say or do. Even the apostle Paul, considered by many to be the most effective and well-known Christian leader in the latter part of the first century, said, "I do what I don't want to do."

The great truth is this: people do not expect you to be perfect at all times in all situations with all people as much as they expect you to face your imperfections, apologize for the hurt you cause others, learn from your mistakes, and alter your course of behavior so that you will do the right thing in the future.

Leadership isn't about perfection. It's about participating in a process that leads to releasing others' perfection. Unforgiveness can definitely be a roadblock to moving forward.

> 2. *Quit it.* State it any way you choose, "Stop it," "End it,"
> "Refuse it," "Get over it." Put an end to the hurtful behavior.

If you are the one being abused or injured, stop allowing yourself to be the victim. Get away from that person— whether he or she your spouse or employer. Say no to the person's behavior. Refuse to be a doormat or to accept the painful wounds that another person is inflicting.

If you are the one dishing out the abuse, stop doing so. Take control over your attitude and behavior. Deal with the anger that causes you to explode all over other people with loud, angry, hurtful remarks. Deal with the cynicism and skepticism that result in your making statements that damage, wound, and discourage others. Deal with the pride that causes you to expect the whole world to bow down to you, and that results in your using people and manipulating people for your own self-satisfaction. Decide that you are no longer going to be a person who needs frequent forgiveness from others!

In facing your emotions and hurt feelings, decide that you are going to get well emotionally. You may need a counselor to help you through the process, or you may need to undertake new disciplines in your life to change the way you think or habitually respond, but do what it takes to say no to bitterness, anger, or hatred.

Quit seeing yourself as a victim. Quit seeing yourself as a whimpering, pouting, suffering person. Quit nursing the hurt. Choose to quit wallowing in the pain.

Quit blaming yourself. You must learn to move past your offenses quickly.

Most people are familiar with the Lord's Prayer. One line in that prayer says, "And forgive us our sins, as we forgive those who sin against us" (Matt. 6:12). Ask yourself, *How do I want to be forgiven?* If possible, wouldn't you choose to be forgiven quickly, completely, and without any further remembrance of or reference to your sin? That is precisely how we must learn to forgive ourselves!

Ask God to help you in the process. In many cases, we can't quit certain emotional habits with just our own willpower. We need His power to go along with the exercise of our wills. Ask God to help you walk away from the person or situation that routinely causes you to live in fear, turmoil, anxiety, or sorrow. Ask God to help you stop hurtful behavior. Ask Him to convict you in advance of your doing the hurtful thing. Ask Him to help you release your hurt feelings and to drain the swamp of anger, bitterness, prejudice, doubt, or hate that you have allowed to become the environment of your soul.

3. *Forget it.* Once you have admitted your sin to God, others, and yourself, and you have repented of your sin and received forgiveness for it, move on. Learn from your experience. Accept God's forgiveness, and forgive yourself. Receive God's help, and then continue to receive His help as you ask for it daily. Choose to go forward in your life.

Forgetting the hurtful situation does not mean that you deny it ever happened. It means that you forget to "remember" that it happened every hour, every day, or every week of your life. Forgetting means that you actively choose not to relive, rehash, or revisit the old conversations or old situations that were damaging to you.

Forgetting the wrong does not mean that you wander forward blindly and without caution or guidance. If you do that, you'll find yourself wandering right into a similar situation in the future! How many people do you know who go from one abusive relationship to another abusive relationship, from one outburst of anger to another, from one act of hateful vengeance to another?

Forgetting means that you let the past be the past as you choose to embrace a different future. You are to learn from what has happened to you, and from what you have done to hurt others. You are to change, to grow, to become something better in the aftermath of a situation that warrants forgiveness.

Forgiveness is not only restorative, it is directive. Genuine forgiveness changes your course—it puts you on a new, upward, better path. It reverses the negative flow in your life and redirects your energy, the application of your skills and talents, and your thought life toward something more positive, beneficial, uplifting, and successful.

Genuine forgiveness says, "I will not go there again. I will not do that again. I will not allow that to be done to me again. I will not subject myself to that again. Instead I will go here, I will do this, I will respond in this way, and I will guard myself or prepare myself in this way."

Forgetting allows you to learn something new. It frees up some of your mental space—the area in which you have been continually reviewing the past and mulling over your possible vengeful response—to engage in creative, new, fresh activities and ideas.

Forgiveness does not mean that you close the door to trusting people or to being vulnerable to people in order to keep yourself from being hurt. Rather, forgiveness means that you adopt new skills, develop a new understanding of faith, renew your mind, and bring healing to your soul so that you can trust and allow yourself to be vulnerable again. Only this time, you trust with eyes wide open, your mind alert, and your heart fortified with huge doses of love, joy, peace, kindness, patience, mercy, and self-control.

Forgetting what lies behind you, you press forward. You pick yourself up, nurse and bandage your cuts and scrapes, allow your brokenness to heal, and get back on the path, not only "recovered" but "renewed."

Releasing Others from Your Heart and Memory

Forgiveness involves more than letting go of hurtful things that people actually do to you. Forgiveness also involves releasing people from your mind and heart for their failure to do what you think they *should* have done.

Many people harbor bitterness and resentment because they think somebody else should have acted in a certain way, helped them in a specific task, or paved the way for them in a better fashion. Many people are seething with deep anger because they do not believe life has played fair with them in the past—their parents didn't do certain things for them; their teachers didn't teach them certain things; their coaches didn't give them certain opportunities.

Let it go. If you are holding on to resentments rooted in what others did not do for you, forgive them for failing you, and walk on. To continue to hold on to that resentment is to fail yourself.

When I was in the fourth grade, my parents divorced. I was never that close to my father, and I don't have a lot of memories related to him. I do remember vividly the day that I was told my parents were divorcing. The first thought that ran through my mind was, *I'm not going to let this affect me.* I don't know how a fourth grader comes up with that conclusion, but I did. And I did not allow their divorce to limit me in my life.

I know a number of adults who are not able to let go of what their parents did to them—directly or indirectly—and who are still shackled by things said to them or done to them when they were children. Some suffer from alcohol and drug abuse. Others are unable to sustain healthy relationships with other people. Many have lives marked by violence that flows from their anger and bitterness. In many cases, these people simply cannot be helped because they do not want to let go of the past.

From my perspective, what seems to happen is this: these people are unable to differentiate other people's lives from their own. They choose to continue to be influenced by what others did and said—they see themselves as inextricably tied to past events or at least to the memory of them. And one result seems to be that they blame their failures today on the actions of others. In many ways, they internalize the failures of their parents (moral failures, character failures, behavioral failures, marital failures) and allow them to become the root of failure in their own lives. In choosing to exert positive influence, you may need to let go of some of the negative influences you have internalized.

Differentiate your experiences, failures, and successes from those of others. See yourself as separate from—yes, even rising above—the failures of others. See yourself as separate from the successes of others; if you don't, you will tend to live in the shadow of those successes and feel yourself less worthy or valuable anytime you do not measure up to what others have achieved. See yourself as separate from the experiences that others have had—the things they have done or said, the places they have gone.

Recognize that your life is *your* life. You may learn from the experiences of others, but no one is to live vicariously, for better or worse, through another person.

You are the gatekeeper of what you allow to influence you. You are the one who determines whether something will be a positive or a negative influence in your life.

Forgiveness: Vital for Personal Greatness

By giving and receiving apologies, you greatly add to understanding, and in building up understanding, you lay the groundwork for all other forms of future influence. A failure to give or receive an apology can become a brick wall to a relationship. Until that wall is hurdled or removed, it is difficult for the relationship to grow.

Giving and receiving forgiveness heals hatred, anger, and bitterness. A failure to forgive can create tensions that erode influence and stifle the pursuit of potential. Until forgiveness is given freely and received fully after a friendship is wounded, the friendship cannot develop further.

Giving and receiving forgiveness is vital to achieving personal greatness. Those who ask for forgiveness send a strong message that although they are not perfect, they desire to grow, change, and move toward perfection. Those who are quick to receive forgiveness send a strong message that they desire for relationships to be healed so that future influence can occur freely and generously.

A forgiving heart is a defining character trait in those who are personally great.

PRODUCING RESULTS

A COMMITMENT TO ACHIEVEMENT

I HAVE A FRIEND NAMED STEVE WHO IS AS GIFTED AND talented as any person I've ever met. He is especially gifted at speaking and at dealing with people. He loves life, he always seems to have fun doing whatever he chooses to do, and in the past, he has had more people dedicated to serving him and working for him than any person I've ever known.

But Steve has never fully figured out who he is. He has identified some of his core values and he has defined some of the principles that guide his behavior, but he has never fully understood or embraced his purpose for being, or hooked that purpose into an even greater cause. He has simply ridden the waves of opportunity that have come his way.

Several years ago, financial adversity rocked Steve's world. Almost overnight, the successful business he had built crumbled. He found himself at the end of a domino-effect chain of business collapses that involved both clients' and loan organizations going bankrupt.

Steve fell apart personally. He became angry and bitter, and he descended into a depression that he would not acknowledge and for which he would not seek help. He left his wife. He stopped calling his grown children. He lost not only his personal fortune and his company, but also many of his friends and virtually all of his business associates.

Steve did well in the "spring seasons" of his life. He was creative, and he knew how to plant new ideas. He did well in the "summer seasons" of his life. He knew how to work hard, pull a plow, and put in extra effort. He did well in the "autumn seasons" of his life. He knew how to reap a harvest, share rewards, and set aside part of the harvest for replanting. But he had absolutely no ability to withstand the isolation and lack of activity in the horrible "winter season" he suddenly experienced.

Today, he remains a depressed, lonely, isolated man. And perhaps the saddest fact of all is that he refuses to be helped or to help himself. He refuses to do the difficult work of determining who he is, why he is on the earth, and what he might still accomplish. Until he changes his thinking from a position of anger at all that life has dished out to him, and begins to adopt instead a position of hope at all that he might still dish up for others, he will likely remain depressed, lonely, and bitter.

I am always puzzled when people say, either by their words or by their actions, "I'm giving up." I do not understand how a person can give up in pursuit of any aspect of his potential.

One of my heroes, Art Williams, used to say, "Everybody wakes up from time to time and feels like quitting. The only difference is that the losers in life really do quit, but the winners do whatever it takes, for as long as it takes, to win."

Why Do You Feel the Way You Do?

If you feel like giving up, or if you believe you have already given up in some area of pursuing your potential, seek to know why. Isolate what has caused your discouragement.

There seem to be five main reasons that people cite for quitting a job. These same reasons seem to be related to why people stop working hard, even though they may remain employed and on the payroll—in other words, why they quit giving their best effort and creativity to an organization:

1. They have suffered some type of devastating blow or set-back (for example, the death of a loved one or the cancellation of a major project in which they have invested years of effort and skill).

   The answer here may lie in counseling or in giving oneself time to heal.

2. They are not being adequately rewarded for the work they are producing. Salary and benefits aren't keeping pace with achievement.

   If you feel this is the cause for your discouragement, you may need to seek a new position in which rewards are greater, or move into a new field in which salaries tend to be higher. More training or skills may be required for you to be successful in a new position or field. In that case, get the training you need!

3. The job moves forward in technology, and they fail to acquire the skills necessary for using the new technology.

In some cases they may not have acquired skills or information in a particular area that is required for advancement.

If this is the reason for your quitting or giving up, go back to school. Get the training you need.

4. They find themselves working in a stifling environment that offers very little praise, recognition, or opportunity for personal initiative.

If you cannot initiate change where you are, seek a place where you are appreciated as a person, you are recognized for your work and experience, and your contributions are valued.

5. They personally are envious of those in authority over them. As a result, they are angry and bitter, and they refuse to give their best effort because they believe to do so is to promote or help someone they don't truly want to succeed.

If this is the cause of your discouragement, adjust your attitude. Either get over feeling angry or bitter, or move on.

What Is Required to Produce Results?

Most people work hard, but significantly fewer produce solid results. Why is that? We have heard that it is better to work smarter rather than harder, but what does that really mean? Just because you are smart, will your efforts be guaranteed to produce superior results?

Producing results requires a commitment to achieving your personal potential and staying focused until you reach your goals. When you truly discover who you are, your efforts will begin to become more focused. Over time, your hard work and focused efforts will produce lasting results.

To a great extent, commitment is a combination of knowing who you are, maintaining your focus on the dreams you have for your life, and making a concerted effort to maximize your God-given potential.

Set Positive Rewards for Yourself

Don't expect all the rewards to be set for you by someone in authority over you. Set some goals for yourself, and establish some rewards for yourself as you reach those goals.

There is a significant difference between people who act simply to avoid negative consequences and those who actively pursue positive rewards.

The employee who shows up at work at the prescribed 8:30 A.M. starting time simply to avoid being written up by a supervisor has a far different mind-set from that of the person who shows up at work an hour early because he's eager to get busy on a job he thoroughly enjoys and finds purposeful and rewarding.

Is it easier for the person to get up and get to work at 7:30 than 8:30? No. I don't care how motivated you are, it's not easier to get a head start on the day. It takes discipline. But it's the right thing to do if you are in hot pursuit of your purpose for living! The person who hits the day hard, and then runs hard all day, can truly say at the end of the day, "I did the right thing today." The person who is lazy, slothful, slow to start, lagging in enthusiasm, paltry in effort, and lackadaisical in terms of quality can never honestly say to himself or others at the end of a day, "I did the right thing today."

Doing the right thing always takes effort. It always takes hard work.

Keep Yourself Motivated

Motivation is like an engine humming inside you. The size of an engine determines how fast that engine is going to be able to propel its load, and how strong that engine is going to be in carrying its intended load.

It's the degree to which you are motivated that will determine how hard you are going to work and how fast you are going to get to the point of feeling rewarded for your work.

Just revving up an engine isn't going to take a person anywhere. You must have a destination point—a set of goals or results toward which you are moving. You also must have three additional items: a steering mechanism, a chassis to carry you, and fuel.

Let's carry the analogy to its simple conclusion. The steering mechanism in your life is your composite set of values and guiding principles—simply put, it is what you believe and how you have chosen to behave. That's what will keep you on the road and maintain your focus on your goal. Your values will allow you to veer around obstacles and stay away from detours that might cause serious damage to your integrity or slow you down.

The chassis is your life—all the many facets of it, including your personality, your likes and dislikes, your style, the family and friends you carry with you in heart and mind, and so forth.

The fuel is your dream, your desire, your sense of "calling" or "destiny." The road map is your plan, and the road is your chosen means of getting from where you are to where you want to be.

That's a very simple analogy, but it's a powerful one.

We tend to spend most of our time pumping gas and polishing our chassis. We dream. We acquire the things we think reflect who we are. We work on our personalities and our friendships and family relationships. All of these things are important. But a freshly polished car full of gas can sit in a driveway and never go anywhere and, in the end, turn into a pile of rust.

Some people study road maps until they are so wrinkled and ripped you can't make out some of the information on them—yet they never actually get in the car and take the trip they have mapped out.

Most of us need to spend more time and give more attention to doing things that cause us to put "the pedal to the metal" and keep our motivation strong. We need to release our motivation into actually going where we desire to go. We need to build ourselves an engine that has enough power to get us there, and to do so with a fair degree of speed and power.

A man who works with me as a consultant on occasion is not only highly qualified, but highly motivated. He is a Vietnam veteran—a marine helicopter pilot—and an engineer. He assumes that every problem has a solution.

Recently we had an appointment with a client in Fayetteville, Arkansas, and Ron found himself stuck in Dallas with every flight to Fayetteville canceled. He jumped into the airport fray, fought his way through the rental car obstacle course, and drove nearly all night so he could make his commitments for the next day. He took the attitude that his presence at the meeting was vital for the meeting to succeed—not necessarily for the meeting to occur, but for the meeting to *succeed.*

Do you have that attitude? Do you see the role you play as being vital? Do you see your contributions as being valuable? If not, why not?

Maintain Your Focus

Nothing of lasting benefit is accomplished unless you maintain focus on the things that are related to your *being*—your talents, values, guiding principles, and life purpose. The more clearly you can define who you are, the more your efforts are likely to come into focus. Over time, your hard work and focused efforts produce lasting results.

Focus can be defined in this way:

F = Find out who you are, and understand your purpose and calling in life.

O = Outline your vision so you can rehearse it to yourself and communicate it to others.

C = Create a plan to achieve your dream.

U = Unify your resources, and apply them to your plan.

S = Stay on course, and determine within yourself that you will weather all adversities.

Some time ago I faced the fact that I needed to lose fifteen pounds. Those pounds had crept on over a year or so. I hadn't been as active as I like to be—in other words, I hadn't played as many rounds of golf as I like to play in a month! I had overindulged in a diet too rich in sweets and fats. It doesn't take much to gain a pound of fat—it takes only an extra 3,200 calories that aren't burned off, and that's about the calorie count in one pint of quality ice cream! No justification, however. I had gained fifteen pounds, and I needed to take them off.

There's a book titled *Stop the Madness*, and I like that title a great deal. It's a phrase I find myself using in my personal life and in my consulting work when bad trends need to be reversed. I needed to stop the madness of my overeating and underexercising.

I made a decision to change the trend and lose the weight.

I made a mental plan for what I needed to do on a daily basis. I needed to walk more, climb more stairs, eat the right things, eat smaller portions of those things, and eliminate desserts. I didn't follow any elaborate diet program. I made a few key decisions that I knew would reduce my calorie count and increase my activity level.

And then I worked the plan patiently, consistently, and diligently. It took a couple of months, but I lost the weight.

I took charge of the problem.

The basics of what I did in this simple single-focus area of my life are the basics of change at any level and in any situation.

First, decide that you are going to do what you know is the right thing to do. Find as many reasons as you may need to motivate yourself to make the decision. Your reason may be rooted in a desire for better health, a better family life, greater financial stability, a stronger spiritual life, or improved friendships. Whatever the reason, it needs to be strong enough and compelling enough that your decision is shored up with firm resolve. A decision is not a whim or a fantasy. It is a declaration of sure intent.

Second, make a plan. The plan need not be elaborate or complicated. Get to the heart of the bad habit you are intending to change. If you want to avoid impulse shopping that tends to drive you into debt, make a plan to stay out of malls and avoid opening mail-order catalogs. Shop with a list. Avoid the shopping channels.

I don't know what the ideal plan might be for you, but I suspect you know the plan. Most people know where they most likely fail to keep a good intention—they know their areas of weakness and the things that trip them up most readily. Make a plan to avoid those places, people, or situations.

Third, work the plan. Refuse to give up, give in, or give way to temptation. Stay steady. Keep moving toward your goal. Reward yourself in positive and healthful ways as you reach goals or subgoals.

MULTIPLE PATHS LEAD TO POSITIVE RESULTS

There's more than one way to accomplish most jobs. There are multiple paths to positive results. Choose the one that works best for you, and don't lock yourself into a methodology or procedure simply because that's the way you've always worked or because that's the traditional approach.

A number of years ago I worked with a client who had something of a hodgepodge of buildings that comprised the corporate campus. As the organization had grown, it had sought to acquire the adjacent turf—literally. It didn't matter if the property was a house, an office building, or a warehouse. Square footage seemed to be the only prerequisite for acquisition. The result was a great deal of wasted, inefficient space and an inefficient means of linking people to results.

The warehouse was a particularly troublesome operation, in my opinion. At the time I began to work with this client, he had almost $1 million worth of stored inventory, much of which he considered to be outdated, unmarketable, or irrelevant to his current message. Nevertheless, he was paying each month to store the material.

The prevailing mind-set of the organization was this: "We need to be able to produce our own products, control every aspect of their production and distribution, and store the products under our roof until the time they are dropped in the mail." The overhead and employee expense for the warehouse alone was about $1 million a year.

We began to discuss the concept of outsourcing the warehousing—in other words, hiring an outside firm to manufacture products as needed, store them in more limited quantities, and distribute them as directed. Such a firm, of course, would be accustomed to manufacturing similar products for several other clients or firms.

I recommended that they sell the current warehouse and eliminate the warehouse staff or assign those employees to other areas that were growing. I recommended the money from the sale of the property be funneled back into company growth.

The net result would be that the company still maintained total control of its message—the creation and design of product. The company would still maintain total control over the mailing list and ordering process, supplying the contracted firm with labels or electronic address data, and requiring the security of data. We anticipated that the company would reap tremendous savings annually.

The plan was put into effect.

In one year, the warehousing operation went from a $1 million expenditure to $60,000. In the wake of that success, we began to outsource other aspects of the company's operation where outsourcing made good sense.

Over a period of several years, many tasks were outsourced, the employee base was streamlined, and new energy and money were released into the development of the company. Key employees were put into place to achieve and maintain agreed-upon results. Tasks were cut back significantly.

At no time did the company lose control of its desired results. Nobody took control over the creative process. Nobody else set the direction of the company's message. It was only in areas of production, manufacturing, and distribution that outsourcing firms were contracted.

At all times, the company maintained control over its vision, goals and results, and the moral climate of its organization. At all times employees were required to stay within the ethical boundaries established by the company, to meet company-established deadlines and budgets, and to follow general procedures established by the corporate administration.

The organization had found a new way to produce results.

If you aren't getting the results you desire in your personal life, take another look at the methodology you are using.

ANOTHER WORD FOR RESULTS: *FRUIT*

Have you ever stopped to seriously consider the fruit of your life? What type of fruit are you producing? What quality? What quantity? Are others being nourished by it?

If I were to go into an orchard in the dead of winter, I doubt that I could tell an apple tree from a pear tree or plum tree. I don't know enough about trees to be able to tell the difference in their general shapes, bark, or limb patterns. In the spring, I might be able to tell the trees apart, but even then, I'm not all that sure about the differences in fruit tree leaves and blossoms. In the summer, however, I can guarantee you that I would be able to distinguish the identity of the trees with 100 percent accuracy because I know the difference between an apple, a pear, and a plum. Furthermore, I could tell you if a piece of fruit is ripe or good to eat, and upon close inspection, if it has insect damage on the inside.

Look at the fruit of your life. What are you producing? What are the character qualities other people can identify in you?

You ultimately will be judged in history—even if it is only the family-lore history told by the next generation at Thanksgiving Day celebrations fifty years from now—by the fruit of your life.

MAKE THE CHOICES THAT LEAD TO FULFILLMENT

A man who exerted strong positive influence in my life once said to me, "Tim, I never told you that what you have chosen to do would be easy. I only told you it would be worth it."

How right he was!

Nothing about what I have chosen to do with my life is easy. I work long hours. I travel thousands of miles a month—sometimes thousands of miles a week. I am away from my family and friends more than I'd like to be. I feel the stress of responsibility for helping others achieve maximum results in their various endeavors. I juggle several projects at any given time, yet I must make every project my number-one priority.

But do I find my purpose in life worth the effort? Absolutely! I wouldn't want to be doing anything else with my life. I can't imagine anything else that could be as personally fulfilling or satisfying, or anything else that would give me as much joy.

Choose to Lead Your Life

Choose to explore your potential, discover and develop your talents, grow in your skills, and exert positive influence. Choose to make decisions based upon your values, purpose, and guiding principles. Choose to develop the "inner you" and to produce results in your "outer world" based upon your deepest beliefs and desires.

Choose to Live a Balanced Life

Those who have studied the life and ministry of Jesus readily know that He spent thirty years growing, as the gospel writer Luke told us, "in wisdom and stature, and in favor with God and men" (Luke 2:52). It was only after He had spent thirty years in those four enterprises—building up His mind, His physical being, His spiritual being, and His relationships with others—that He moved out into His life's work and had the power and spiritual authority to turn water into wine, which was His first miracle.

What are you doing today to build yourself up mentally and grow in wisdom? Are you growing in physical health? Are you growing in your relationship with God? Are you growing in your relationships with others? These four areas of life are intended to be in balance, and all are intended to work together in strength.

Only you can determine the balance of your life. Only you can decide how you will set priorities, govern your time, and expend your energy. Only you can decide how you will exert influence—as well as where, when, to whom, and for what purposes. Choose to lead a balanced life that is focused and highly motivated.

Choose to Be Great

I encourage you to seek personal greatness. I encourage you to *want* to be great. I encourage you to see yourself as a person of potential, talents, and influence.

Give your best effort to being your best self.

Give your best energies to producing your best work.

Give your best skills to good deeds that will influence others to pursue their greatness.

Unlock your potential and exert positive influence with all of your talents and abilities, heart, mind, soul, and will, and you *will* achieve personal greatness. I guarantee it.

ABOUT THE AUTHOR

TIM LAVENDER IS THE FOUNDER OF LEADERS FOR LIFE and President of Nextlevel Consulting. For the last twenty-five years, Lavender has specialized in building leaders and developing organizations, working with Fortune 500 companies and major nonprofit organizations. He speaks to thousands each year through Leaders for Life seminars on the subjects of leadership, building people, and building organizations.

MORE BESTSELLING BOOKS ON LEADERSHIP
FROM THOMAS NELSON PUBLISHERS

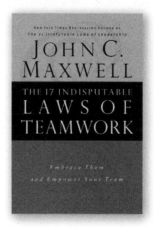

EVERYONE WHO WORKS WITH PEOPLE IS REALIZING that the old autocratic method of leadership simply doesn't work. The way to win is to build a great team.

John C. Maxwell has been teaching the benefits of leadership and team building for years. Now he tackles the importance of teamwork head-on, writing about teamwork being necessary for every kind of leader, and showing how team building can improve every area of your life.

Written in the style of the best-seller *The 21 Irrefutable Laws of Leadership*, this new book not only contains laws that you can count on when it comes to getting people to work together, but it presents them in such a way that you can start applying them to your own life today. And it's illustrated with great stories of team leaders—and team breakers—from history, business, the church, and sports.

ISBN 0-7852-7434-0

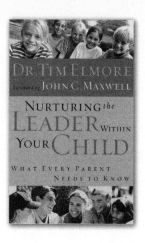

HOW DO I BRING OUT THE BEST IN MY CHILD? WHAT can I do to help my children reach their full potential? Why is it important to encourage leadership in my child? John Maxwell protégé Dr. Tim Elmore answers these questions and others in *Nurturing the Leader Within Your Child.* Using a survey of over 3,000 students, he enters the minds of today's youth to understand their desire to affect their world, their way.

Beginning with a foreword by John C. Maxwell, the book is in four unique sections (What You Need to Know, What They Need to Know, When to Seize the Moment, How to Pass it On). Dr. Elmore gives practical tools for bridging the generation gap to foster character and growth in your children. Offering a list of fundamental qualities every leader must possess, Dr. Elmore helps parents and youth workers recognize teachable moments and equips them to structure an individual mentoring plan for each child. Finally, he offers evaluation methods for recognizing progress.

ISBN 0-7852-6614-3

MISSION

We focus the energy of our lives on passionately seeking out emerging leaders, helping them develop the incredible potential that lies within and find the pathway that leads for a lifetime.

GUIDING PRINCIPLES

- We believe that leadership can change the world.

- We believe there is incredible potential that lies within emerging leaders.

- We believe in being intoxicated by the success of others.

- We believe in the life-changing power of building relationships that endure for a lifetime.

- We believe that it is the development of both character and competency that creates great leaders.

- We believe that true leaders learn how to transcend hard work to produce superior results.

- We believe that real leaders learn how to do what is right and tell the truth.

- We believe that building great organizations is a product of building great people.

PROMISE

We will help you find the pathway that leads for a lifetime.

For more infomation, please contact Info@Leadersforlife.com
www.LeadersforLife.com